# THE SAGA OF KOSOVO
## FOCUS ON
## SERBIAN—ALBANIAN RELATIONS

ALEX N. DRAGNICH

AND SLAVKO TODOROVICH

EAST EUROPEAN MONOGRAPHS, BOULDER

DISTRIBUTED BY COLUMBIA UNIVERSITY PRESS, NEW YORK

1984

EAST EUROPEAN MONOGRAPHS, NO. CLXX

# CONTENTS

## MAPS

**Prince Lazar's Coat of Arms**

(Sketch by Zoran Jovanovich)

# PREFACE

As an aid to the reader, we offer a brief explanation concerning our choices of some terminology and stylistic usages. We have kept references in the text to a minimum, but we call attention to our selected bibliography and to the annotated index. As an aid to pronunciation, instead of using diacritical marks over certain letters, we have added letters so as to approach the correct phonetic sound. The only exceptions: when to do so would change the beginning letter of a name or place, and where a name is a direct part of the cited work. We have kept capitalization to a minimum. The words communism and communist have been capitalized only when the reference is clearly to the party or to communist rulers. Inclusive dates after the name of early Serbian rulers, or other high officials, indicate the years of rule. Dates after place names, notably historic monuments, indicate the approximate years of their construction.

We often speak of Serbia and Montenegro and of Serbs and Montenegrins. It should be kept in mind that Montenegrins are Serbs, and in their earliest history Serbs and Montenegrins were one nation. As historical developments took their course, however, two Serbain states (Serbia and Montenegro) evolved and were again united only in 1918. It is therefore more convenient and, we believe, less confusing to adhere to the historical designations. Moreover, post-World War II Yugoslav rulers created Montenegro as one of six Yugoslav republics, and in population statistics they have insisted on Montenegrin as a distinct and separate national group.

When speaking of Yugoslav Albanians we have occasionally used the word *Schipetars* (Shiptari in Serbo-Croatian), a term which has been in popular usage among Yugoslav citizens. Some Yugoslavs, as well as other Slavs, have continued to use the Turkish term *Arnaut* for persons of Albanian nationality. In Albania, that country is today referred to as *Shqiperi* and its inhabitants as *Shqipetari*. Many Western authors refer to them as *Shkipetari* or *Schipetari*. We have preferred to employ the term Albanian or Schipetars.

Finally, we have attempted to be objective, but we have not pretended to be exhaustive. The latter would have been impossible in a brief book that covered several centuries. We have sought to follow a common thread that we considered important and interesting. The extent to which we have succeeded in this effort at popular history writing, only the reader will be in a position to judge.

A. N. D.
S. P. T.

Krushevats

Zhicha

Milesheva          Studenitsa
      Sopochani

Patriarchate      Trepcha
      Pech         Prishtina
Dubrovnik   Kotor   Grachanitsa   Novo
          Dechani               Brdo
               Prizren      Skoplje

          Debar

        Ohrid

ADRIATIC                Salonika

                              Hilandar

            Serres

Key to Boundaries

━━━  Nemanja's Serbia After 1191

----  Tsar Dunshan's Serbia, 1331-
                              1355                AEGEAN

                              Map by Cynthia Stilwill

   Medieval Serbia

# INTRODUCTION

In March and April 1981, large-scale disturbances broke out in Yugoslavia's autonomous province of Kosovo, which is part of the Republic of Serbia but populated mainly by people who look upon themselves as Albanians. The riots were spearheaded by students from the province's university in the city of Prishtina. The disorders originated in the cafeteria, allegedly as a demonstration protesting the poor quality of the food served to the students. Within a few days demonstrations not only occurred in other parts of Prishtina, but in several other Kosovo cities as well. More important, however, was the fact that they took on a political cast, with slogans that suggested disaffection with Yugoslavia and a desire to unite with Albania. The riots were put down with an indeterminate loss of life.

Although the problem of Kosovo is complex and complicated, for about one-half of Yugoslavia's population, the Serbs, it is not. To them Kosovo is holy ground. It is the cradle of their nationhood, when they were virtually its sole occupants. It was the center of Serbia's empire of the middle ages, at one time the strongest empire in the Balkans. It was in Kosovo in 1389 that Ottoman forces won the crucial battle with the Serbs, leading to the end of their empire. But Kosovo is also the place where Serbia's most historic and religious monuments are located.

1

To understand today's Kosovo and its problems, as well as how it relates to Yugoslavia's relations with Albania, and even to the possibility of foreign, including Soviet, intervention under certain conditions, it is necessary to know what happened in the area during the intervening centuries of Turkish rule, when the Serbs could do little more than seek to preserve Kosovo as a symbol of their identity, their greatness, and the hope of their ultimate resurrection.

Our story begins at the time when the two branches of Christendom—the Catholic Church of Rome and the Orthodox Christians of Constantinople—were at each others throats, unable to find common ground. The Eastern Empire (Byzantium) lost Asia Minor to the Turks (1071) of the Seljuk tribe. This meant an equally disastrous blow to the Western world, because it affected the profitable trade routes to the markets of the Far East. Venice, Pisa, and Genoa had an extensive commercial interest in those routes. Under the excuse of fighting the "Eastern heresy" and the "saving of Christ's burial places," Western crusaders found their way to Byzantine treasures, conquering Constantinople in 1204, and breaking up Byzantium into three states Epirus, Trebizond, and Nicea. This is when Serbia emerged as an independent state, subsequently an empire.

In 1261, Byzantine leader Michael Palaeologus finally succeeded in recapturing Constantinople, but the restored empire lacked its former strength. With the old foes (Latins) still around, plus the rise of the Slavs (Serbs and Bulgars), the Byzantines turned to the Turks for help, only to see the Turks at the walls of Constantinople (1359), their victory over the Serbs at Kosovo (1389), and their taking of Constantinople (1453).

For our purposes, it is necessary to have some picture of what happened under the rule of the Ottoman Turks, who subsequently were to reach the gates of Vienna. It is also useful to have some picture of how Serbia managed its resurrection in the nineteenth century, and how it liberated

Kosovo in the Balkan wars (1912). And it is also essential to have some appreciation of the impact of World War I and subsequent attempts to deal with the question of Kosovo.

In addition, it is imperative to understand how World War II affected Kosovo, and how the Yugoslav Marxists proposed to deal with the problem of nationalities, and how they "solved" the Kosovo question.

Finally, we shall look at the nature of Yugoslav Communist rule in Kosovo and some of its consequences. At that point we shall raise some questions about the future, speculate about Kosovo's destiny, as well as examine the possible impact of what happens in Kosovo upon international relations, including those of the great powers.

# CHAPTER I

## KOSOVO AND MEDIEVAL SERBIA

Kosovo is many diverse things to different living Serbs, but they all have it in their blood. They are born with it. The variety of meanings is easily explained by the symbolism and emotions that the word "Kosovo" embodies, clearly above anything that the geographic concept might imply. The question of why it is in Serbian blood is never meant to be answered—it is a transcendental phenomenon.

Serbs with a visual memory of the Kosovo region see it as a somewhat sleepy valley, whose surrounding hills, in their descent, seem to have overstretched. Some 4,200 square miles in size (with an additional 2,000 square miles of adjacent Metohija), this cradle of the Serbian nation is carried by two broad-shouldered gentle giants, somber and dark Mount Kopaonik in the north and white-capped and fair Mount Shar in the south.

Kosovo, comparatively, is good pasture land as well as corn, wheat, and fruit land. Yet Kosovo peasants can barely scratch out a subsistence tilling the clayish soil that is exposed to winds that dry the ground. For these peasants Kosovo provides a lean and meager lot.

To others Kosovo is a breadbasket. To those who descended from the slopes of the mountains, or who came there from poorer regions as homesteaders, Kosovo seems a promised land.

Kosovo is a bottomless ancient mining pit, rich in zinc, lead, and silver, but it is not a melting pot.

Kosovo is a plain where the Serbs bend over to work the soil, Albanians sweat in the mining shafts underground, Turks (largely spent and reminiscing about past fame) grow poppies and peppers, while the Gypsies fill the air with the sounds of life.

To the Serbs, that plain of suffering, of want, and of sacrifice is Holy Ground. They come there to clench their fists and shout at the earth where dead Turks lie. As Rebecca West has written: "Dead Christians are in Heaven, or ghosts, not scattered lifeless bones. . .only Turks perish thus utterly."

The Lord Almighty, some might say, must have predestined Kosovo as a battlefield, a rendezvous for hostile earthly encounters. It is a junction that led many a nation astray, if not to a dead end. Byzantines, Bulgars, Serbs, Magyars, Austrians, Albanians, and Turks—all marched through it at certain times, but in a sense got nowhere. Kosovo seems as nature's boxing ring where world ideologies—Christian, Bogumil, Moslem, and more recently Marxist—each won individual rounds, but not the fight. This plain seems to have attracted strategists of all faiths, who came as dragons sounding their bugles and shouting their battle cries. There must have been six major human slaughters in as many centuries on this peaceful stretch of land. The soil in this valley appears to have fed on human flesh and blood.

Kosovo is that heartbreaking medieval embroidery made in 1402, in the stillness of the Serbian monastery Ljubostinja, with the needle of the pious Serbian princess Euphemia. She sketched her Requiem in gold thread on a pall to cover the severed head of Prince Lazar: "In courage

and piety did you go out to do battle against the snake
Murad . . . your heart could not bear to see the hosts of
Ismail rule Christian lands. You were determined that if
you failed you would leave this crumbling fortress of
earthly power and, red in your own blood, be one with
the hosts of the heavenly King. . . . "

Kosovo is a grave and a grave means death and dust, but
it also means rebirth and a source of new life. Kosovo is
thus transcendental.

What does the reader know of the nation (medieval
Serbia) that was once laid in the Kosovo grave? The one
that stares at us from monastery walls under heavy layers
of soot? The one that watches from under those thick
curved eyebrows? The one with eyes that, when occasionally visited by inquisitive sun rays, refuse to squint? The
eyes of the nation that over the centuries withstood the
Moslem stare, and perished without ever blinking, and
once lifeless was left without anyone to pull the lids down?

Serbia as a nation came into its own sometime in the
eleventh century, in the center of the Balkan peninsula,
which at that time was within the vast realm of the mighty
Byzantine Empire. A lighthouse between two continents,
Constantinople in those days was a beacon light for all
sorts of wayfarers: those in submission, those in power,
those in revolt, those hungry for culture, those driven by
greed. As any potentate, Constantinople at that time had
no friends in the whole world.

Byzantium had very little reason to cherish the Slavs in
the Balkan areas, Serbs or Bulgars, because they proved to
be a nuisance from the time of their arrival, together with
or before the marauding Avars. To Byzantium, incursions
of barbarians were no big problem, for even when they ransacked the walled cities they soon left. Slavs, on the other
hand, inherently were not nomadic types. Once having arrived they tended to settle, and by doing so they changed
the ethnic character of the area.

Byzantine rulers, especially Emperor Basil II, tried to drive the Slavs out, especially the Bulgars, but in the long run arrogancy gave way to political realism, which forced the ever more insecure Byzantine emperors to accept Serbs and Bulgars as permanent inhabitants of the Balkan peninsula. In time they learned to deal with the Slavs on equal or almost equal terms, partly because there were more serious problems confronting them. There were the Persians, Moslem Arabs, and Seljuk Turks, who kept the Byzantines occupied in the East for several centuries. In the West the Normans and the Venetians were sapping Byzantium's military strength. The Slavs, for their part, exploited these troubles to expand and solidify their positions. Even after Constantinople managed to restore much of its imperial prestige, it was challenged in the North by the invading Magyars, who waged four successive wars against Byzantium.

This presented the Serbian ruler of Rascia (Nemanja—1168-1196) an opportunity not to be missed. He moved quickly toward Serbian recognition and independence. It was not an easy task, and he was not continually successful in the process. There was a time when his supporters, Hungary and Venice, could not help him. Facing the angry Manuel I alone, Nemanja was defeated and taken a prisoner to Constantinople, where he was led through the streets with a rope around his neck, to the wild enjoyment of the crowds. It must be remembered that protocol and symbolism meant a great deal in Byzantine culture, so that when Nemanja was brought to submission he had to present himself barefooted and bareheaded, offering his sword and prostrating himself on the ground.

Since Rascia was under the overlordship of Byzantium, Manuel thought that this humiliation of an unfaithful prince would be enough and let Nemanja return to his people. In addition, Nemanja was forced to pay tribute and to provide auxiliary (support) troops. What really may have saved Nemanja's life was the proximity of Rascia (which by that time had already merged with Zeta, another Serbian principality) to the Western world. After all, at that time Christendom was seriously endangered by Islam, and the Emperor badly needed the support of the West, and even of those annoying Slavs in the Balkans.

It should also be noted that when the Westerners march-ed toward Jerusalem the natural route was through the Morava valley which was inhabited by the Slavs. As a mat-ter of fact when one of the leaders of the Third Crusade (Barbarossa) came through there in 1189, Nemanja met him at the border of Rascia and proposed that he forget about Jerusalem and instead occupy Constantinople, but at that moment Barbarossa was not interested.

Byzantine rulers, for their part, did not know whom to trust. And in the confused evolution of developments, Nemanja sought to exploit the situation. He played the Latin world against the Greek, and in the process obtained from the West political recognition for Rascia and a crown for his son Stefan. A papal delegate delivered the crown in 1217. Soon thereafter Stefan the First-Crowned turned East, to the Patriarch of Nicea, and obtained ecclesiastical independence for Rascia. This was in fact the work of his brother Rastko (Monk Sava), who was ordained the first native Serbian archbishop. All Serbs know that Sava began the illustrious line of Serbian archbishops and patriarchs who led the Serbian church and people through subsequent dark times, when the Moslem curtain had fallen upon the Balkans.

Rascia (now Kingdom of Serbia) continued its rise. After spreading its wings, Rascia never ceased being the nucleus of the nation. The small river that supposedly gave the name to Rascia is part of the Ibar river basin, located a few miles north of Kosovo. The capital of Rascia was the city of Ras, which was in the vicinity of today's Novi Pazar. The precise location of Ras has never been positively estab-lished. Some believed it to be at the location of Eski (Old) Pazar, but no ruins were found. The historian Jirecek, who is considered the outstanding authority on medieval Balkan affairs, maintains that Ras was the same place as the one called "Trgovishte," an important commercial center and caravan station used by Dubrovnik merchants until 1445, when the Turks built Novi Pazar.

Another important Serbian town was Dezhevo, from the name of the rivulet Dezhevka (left tributary of the river Rashka). It was built around the Royal Court to replace the antiquated facility at Ras. This is the place where in 1282 King Stefan Dragutin, ruler of the northern regions of Serbia and Srem, abdicated in favor of his brother, King Stefan Milutin (1282-1321), who until then had ruled the southwestern parts of Serbia.

In the immediate vicinity of Ras and Dezhevo are the well-known old Serbian monasteries of Sopochani and Djurdjevi Stubovi.

It is interesting that Serbian medieval documents use the terms "Rascian Lands" and "Rascian King" only in a few instances. Serbs nearly always referred to their territories as Serbian lands, especially in the post-Nemanja period. Merchants and diplomats from the coast city republic of Dubrovnik, who maintained close links with Serbian authorities and courts, used Vatican nomenclature and called Serbia "Sclavonia," although subsequently they adopted the term "Serbia."

The inhabitants of Dubrovnik, those that knew the language, felt very much at home in Serbia, but they had their good and bad days there. Because the two main caravan routes to Constantiniple passed through Serbian territories, custom bills were due to Serbian rulers, complaints were filed, requests for protection or bailing out of jail submitted, down payments made, and court cases litigated. Thanks to all the resulting documents, filed in the Dubrovnik archives, historians have been able to reconstruct the fabric of life in Medieval Serbia.

Serbian rulers, in a manner of speaking, were seeking to pursue a "non-aligned" policy. On the one hand, they fought Byzantium but could never rid themselves of its spell. Although Serbia was never governed directly by Byzantium, as the well-known Byzantologist, George Ostrogorski, says: ". . . it is impossible to separate its medieval history from Byzantium." This should not be understood, however, as cultural assimilation. After all, Constantinople was *the* cultural capital of the world at that time. No wonder that young emerging neighboring states should look to it as an example.

At times the Serbs were successful in their struggle against Byzantium. Tsar Dushan (1331-1355), whose formative years were spent in Constantinople during his father's exile there, conquered half of it (Macedonia, Epirus, Thessaly), and made Serbia the strongest empire in the Balkans. Serbia's territory in Dushan's time covered the vast area from the Danube, the lower Adriatic, and the Aegean. He signed his edicts: "Emperor and Autocrat of the Serbs, Byzantines, Bulgars, and Albanians."

Dushan did not hide his claim to the throne of Byzantium. In 1345, he conquered Serres, the city in Greece on the road to Constantinople. He wanted the powerful Greek clergy in Byzantium to recognize him. When the patriarch at Constantinople hesitated to crown him, he summoned the Serbian and Bulgarian bishops for a council at Skoplje. The bishops raised the autocephalous Serbian archbishopric of Pech to the rank of Patriarchate (1346), and in less than a month the newly-elected Serbian Patriarch (Joanikije II) crowned Stefan Dushan emperor.

Dushan may have grown up in Constantinople, but he also sought approval in the West, notably from Venice and the Papacy, suggesting that he be regarded as "Captain of Christendom." To be sure, Dushan had subjugated the center of Byzantine Christianity, Mount Athos. Apart from Constantinople, this finger-shaped peninsula (south of Salonika) on which Mount Athos stands was the most active spiritual and cultural center of Byzantium. This oasis of poverty, chastity, and obedience—the three vows that

every monk was required to take—was a beacon that attracted souls yearning for peace and education. Secular
Balkan leaders at times found this a reservior of skillful
hands and brilliant minds from which they recruited.

Dushan travelled to visit the Serbian monastery (Hilandar) on Mount Athos, together with his wife Jelena, a
feat in itself, because no female (human or animal) was
ever permitted to set foot on the peninsula of Mount Athos.
Today, as one visits Hilandar and walks the path leading
from the small harbor to the monastery there is a stone
cross-like monument where allegedly Empress Jelena
heard the voice of the Blessed Mother, warning her not to
enter the monastery but to stay put where she was. Even
the monks who tell you this story today shake their heads
in reverent awe and say: "I wonder who would have dared
say that to Dushan the Mighty!"

The influence of the Romanized world, on the other
hand, was far from negligible, and at times a source of great
tension. In the entourage of Serbian kings, Roman Catholic courtiers, German guards, and foreign ladies wed to
Serbian kings tried to interject tidbits of Latin style, fash-
ion and mores. The best Serbian appreciation of Romanized
culture is Stefan Dechanski's (1321-1331) beautiful monastery church of Dechani, built by a Franciscan friar and
Dalmatian stone masons, with fresco works by the Kotor
school artists. It is known, however, that both King Milutin
and later Stefan Dechanski's son, Tsar Dushan, were occasionally annoyed by the Western influence but tolerated
it.

Most of Dushan's imperial time was spent in the Hellenic
area of his realm. Knowing Greek, he felt pretty much at
home there, leaving central Serbia in the care of his son
Urosh. Dushan replaced the Greek aristocracy with Serbian
administrators, his comrades in arms, and gave them Byzantine titles. This could not have pleased the inhabitants, but
Dushan was more interested in courting the Venetians, who
could give him the ships necessary to take Constantinople.

But to the Roman Catholic West Dushan was and remained an "Eastern Schismatic" who was not to be trusted. In a sense they were right, because Dushan was seeking to shape the culture of his realm through the use of the Serbian clergy and nobility, recruited from the Serbian peasantry, anti-Western as much as anti-Eastern.

\* \* \* \*

Serbia of the Nemanjich dynasty was without doubt a land of economic and cultural progress that surpassed the existing European average. Apart from the well-known monasteries and their impressive frescos there are smaller but masterly art objects from that era: golden cups and challices, candlesticks and silver plates, jeweled reliquaries, delicate embroideries, book bindings, and artistic illuminations—produced by talented people in a society which gave them an opportunity to express themselves. As for the Serbian rulers, unlike those in the West, they did not build enduring castles, but each one of them felt duty bound to build at least one monastery.

In the legal-governmental sphere, Tsar Dushan's Code of Laws (Zakonik), studiously prepared over a period of about six years (1349-1354), is recognized to be among the leading law systems of the world.

Moreover, Medieval Serbia was also a part of the international community, relating on a state to state basis in matters of political, military, and cultural importance. Serbian royal courts communicated on levels of respect and honor with Venetian Doges, Hungarian Kings, Bulgarian Tsars, and Byzantine Emperors. Moreover, they were connected through marital arrangements with most of them. The first wife of Stefan the First-Crowned was Eudocia, daughter of Byzantine Emperor Alexis III. King Stefan Urosh I married the French princess Helene (House of Anjou), and Stefan Dragutin married Katherine, daughter of Hungarian King Stephen V, just to name a few.

It is only natural that a society with its own alphabet, language, state, and autocephalous church, should have the urge to create its own literature and culture. A large body of Western medieval literature, such as the Old and New Testaments, liturgical books, theological treatises, dogmatic and apochryphal works, chronicles and life stories of the saints, was there either in the original or in translation. And major medieval novels, such as the tales about Alexander the Great, Tristan and Isolda, were also known. But this was not enough. The need to have their own literature was strongly felt by Serbian rulers and their associates.

Among the Serbian medieval literati were ecclesiastics and laics. Two of them were of royal blood, although technically not because Nemanja was not crowned (Nemanja's two sons, Stefan and Rastko-Sava—a rare case in the world's history), and one was of noble princely heritage (Prince Lazar's son Despot Stefan). Others were of peasant stock, educated as monks or priests. Still others were foreign born, highly educated, who found cultural refuge in Serbian courts or monasteries. The very proximity to the great Hellenic culture, almost guaranteed that many cultured men would be roaming the Balkan spaces.

Monastics, courtiers, and a maze of Slavic-speaking subjects of Venice, Byzantium, Hungary, and Bulgaria swarmed around Serbian literary centers. Knowing the Serbian language was an asset in other than literary activities. Venice and Byzantium, and later the Turks, quickly discovered that interstate and other correspondence was likely to be most efficient if carried out in Serbian.

One of those yearning for peace and education was the Serbian Prince Rastko (Sava), Nemanja's youngest son, mentioned above. Clandestinely he left the court. One stormy night he banged on the heavy wooden gates of a Mount Athos monastery (Panteleimon), pleading with the monks to let him in, and save him from the inclement weather and a posse. He was admitted, and began to study theology, languages, and history. His aging father subsequently joined him, and purchased an old ruin where the building of the Serbian monastery Hilandar was begun a short time before he fell ill and died.

The respectful son later wrote a biography of his beloved
father, the founder of the dynasty and Serbian statehood.
He titled it, *The Life of Master Simeun,* a work dealing with
with the secular Nemanja but with the spiritual Simeun,
the monk of noble heritage. In addition to a profusion of
translated church manuals, canonic and instructive texts
for use by Serbian monks and priests back home, Sava also
tried his hand at verse writing. Being the most traveled Serb
of his time, Sava visited and personally knew several Byzantine emperors (Alexis III, Theodor Lasker, John Vatatzes,
Theodor Angelicus), and the patriarchs of Constantinople
(Athanasius) and of Nicea (Manuel). Sava knew the frailty
of men, the mighty and the weak. In a poem, entitled
"Word about Torment," he writes:

> Dead am I even before my death,
> I sentence myself even before the judge does.
> Even before the ceaseless pain sets in,
> I am already tortured by my own agony.

Sava's brother, King Stefan the First-Crowned (1196-
1228) also  wrote a biography of his father. But being occupied with matters of state, he had little time for spiritual
preoccupations, and hence his biography is written from
the point of view of a dynast, national ruler, protector of
the faith, and statesman. While Sava had been of invaluable
help to his brother in consulting about national affairs, he
did not write about it. Stefan began writing the biography
after Nemanja's body had been brought to Serbia (Studenitsa Monastery) in 1208 and finished it in 1216. Other
Serbian writers later wrote about Nemanja, but none with
such a wealth of detail and so informatively.

Subsequently, a new generation of Serbian authors wrote
about Sava and King Stefan, particularly the monks Dom-
entian and Theodosius (second half of the 13th century),
both of the Hilandar school. There were authors who attained high ecclesiastical posts, such as Archbishop Danilo

II (1324-1338), who personally knew three Serbian kings (Dragutin, Milutin, and Stefan Dechanski). He wrote a historical essay on the "Lives of Serbian Kings and Bishops." His poem, "The Lament of Bulgarian Soldiers for Tsar Mihail," is a part of every Serbian anthology (Mihail was Stefan's father-in-law, killed in the battle of Velbuzhd, 1330, the battle that ended Bulgarian primacy among Slavs in Byzantium). Among Serbian medieval patriarchs, the best of the literati was Danilo III (elected at the council of Zhicha, 1390), who together with Lazar's widow Militsa and her children, transported the body of the beheaded Prince from Prishtina to the Ravanitsa Monastery and canonized Lazar to Sainthood.

As for Lazar's son, Despot Stefan (1389-1427), he was an exceptional man indeed. A dashing man of war, letters, and politics, he was the hero of the Battle of Angora (Asia Minor, 1402), where he fought as a Turkish vassal for Bayazet, the killer of his father. Of the three Serbian vassals in Turkish ranks at the earlier battle of Rovine (in Wallachia in 1395 against Prince Mircea), Stefan was the only one who survived. The popular King Marko of Prilep and Konstantin Dejanovich of Eastern Macedonia perished. Despot Stefan was a great benefactor, protector of refugees, writers, and artists. A humanist of wide culture, he was also an author in his own right. One of his poetic scripts is entitled: "Love Surpasses Everything, and No Wonder Because God Is Love." Another was the "Ode to Prince Lazar," a beautiful text chiseled in the marble column which was placed at the spot of the Kosovo battle. A third, "An Ode to Love," was dedicated to his brother Vuk, whom he once fought at that very field of Kosovo. In Stefan's monastery, Resava, generations of monks, scribes and artists have worked tediously to preserve the Serbian heritage (the famous Morava school).

A great patriot and Serbian nationalist, Stefan Lazarevich had the misfortune of presiding over the declining days of his beloved country. Had he been Dushan's successor instead

of Lazar's, the history of the Serbian people might have
been different. At a crucial time when Serbia had a chance
to outmatch Byzantium, Dushan's son Urosh ruled (1355-
1371). He was a weakling, lacking the necessary firmness
and general leadership qualities. The respect and awe that
Stefan commanded among the Turks and Tartars at Angora,
when he rode at the head of three gallant charges against
Tamerlane, in an effort to save his surrounded suzerain,
speaks of the effect his presence might have had if he had
inherited the throne in 1355, when Dushan died.

Today, with the benefit of hindsight, we can see it clearly,
but could King Vukashin and Despot Uglesha even have
anticipated Kosovo? Could the Hungarian kings have fore-
seen Mohacs? Could John VI Cantacuzenus have known
what he was doing to himself, to Byzantium, and to the
Christian world, by leaning on the support of his powerful
but dangerous Moslem ally? And the countries of the West,
could they have known what their insistence on ecclesiastical submission to Rome, as a price of aid, would lead to?

When in desperation, Byzantine Emperor Manuel II beg-
ged for assistance from the Pope, the Doge, the kings of
France, England, and Aragon, his plea for help in fighting
against the "infidels" went unanswered. The Emperor spent
several years on this tragic mission to Venice, Paris, London, and other cities. The trip was full of pageantry and
had a certain cultural importance in terms of the early
renaissance education, but from a political point of view it
meant only vague promises that remained unfulfilled. Reconciliation between East and West, the Greek and Latin
worlds, Eastern Orthodoxy and Catholicism, were out of
the question. The two sides would not attempt to do together what they were unable to achieve alone, i.e., to stop
the Turks. One wonders, would there have been two sieges
of Vienna (1529 and 1683), if Roman Catholic Europe
had come to the aid of the Eastern Orthodox Emperor
(Dushan) in the 1350s.

Even the defeats at Nicopolis (town in Bulgaria on the Danube, 1396), and Varna (1444), which wiped out all hopes for Christendom to clear the Balkans of Islam, could not bring unity. After Nicopolis, Hungarian King Sigismund and a motely crew of French and German knights barely saved their lives, in an escape that took them all the way through the Dardanelles. As they sailed through the narrows, the Christian captives were lined up along the banks, on the order of the Sultan, and made to shout at their humiliated leaders. And at Varna, the Christian leaders did not have an opportunity to flee: King Vladislav of Hungary and Poland, and the Pope's delegate, Cardinal Julian Cesarini, fell òn the field. Djurdje Brankovich, the last of the Serbian despots and a weak member of the Christian coalition, realized even before Varna that the coalition's chance for success were poor, and withdrew. This did not help, however, the Despotate, which succumbed in 1459, six years after Constantinople fell to the Turks (1453). The black two-headed eagle of Byzantium moved to Moscow to become the symbol of the "Third Rome," nourishing the fancy of Balkan Slavs for centuries to come.

# CHAPTER II

## THE KOSOVO BATTLE

Of all Kosovo battles only one counts in the formation of the psyche of a Serb. It is the one that began in the early hours of Vidovdan (St. Vitus Day), June 15, 1389 (June 28 new calendar). The Turks had already been on the European continent for some time, seemingly unstoppable and intoxicated by easy victories over the rival and disunited "infidels."

The battle of Kosovo took place on the part of the Kosovo plain that the Turks called Mazgit, where the rivulet Lab flows into the river Sitnica. Today's visitors learn where Sultan Murad's intestines were buried, where the Turkish standard bearer (Gazimestan) fell, where grateful Serbia erected a "Memorial to the fallen heroes of Kosovo," and where a marble column once stood (placed there on the order of, and authored by, Prince Lazar's son, Despot Stefan Lazarevich), which had the following inscription:

> Oh man, stranger or hailing from this soil, when you enter this
> Serbian land, whoever you may be . . . when you come to this
> field called Kosovo, you will see all over it plenty of bones of
> the dead, and with them myself in stone nature, standing up-
> right in the middle of the field, representing both the cross and

18

the flag. So as not to pass by and overlook me as something unworthy and hollow, approach me, I beg you, oh my dear, and study the words I bring to your attention, which will make you understand why I am standing here. . . . At this place there once was a great autocrat, a world wonder and Serbian ruler by the name of Lazar, an unwavering tower of piety, a sea of reason and depth of wisdom . . . who loved everything that Christ wanted. . . . He accepted the sacrificial wreath of struggle and heavenly glory. . . . The daring fighter was captured and the wrath of martyrdom he himself accepted . . . the great Prince Lazar. . . . Everything said here took place in 1389 . . . the fifteenth day of June, Tuesday, at the sixth or seventh hour, I do not know exactly, God knows.

Following World War II, a redesigned monument was erected, a 25 meter tall tower, together with about 25 acres of the surrounding land, where the famous Kosovo peonies supposedly sprout from the blood of the Kosovo heroes.

The Serbian army was encamped along the right bank of the Lab, an area suitable for both infantry and cavalry troops. The right wing of the Serbian army was under the command of Vojvoda Dimitrije Vojinovich. The left wing stood under the command of Vojvoda Vlatko Vukovich, sent by Bosnian King Tvrtko. Prince Lazar kept the command of the center for himself. The reserve was under the command of Prince Lazar's son-in-law, Vojvoda Vuk Brankovich.

Prince Lazar had many reasons to worry about the outcome of the forthcoming encounter. Murad gave him no time to rally his vassals and tributary lords, some of whom were conspicuously slow in marshaling their troops. Lazar's frantic efforts to obtain help from allies such as the king of Hungary, failed because it was difficult, if not impossible, to organize it on such short notice. Nevertheless, although ill-prepared, Lazar had no other choice but to face the enemy. Murad's advisers, a group of extremely skilled military veterans, insisted on immediate and fast action. Amassed in the area of today's Nish and Kumanovo, the Turkish generals were eager to meet the Serbs while still possessing the momentum of previously victorious campaigns.

Morale in the Serbian camp was not high. Lazar's commanders were torn apart by local rivalries, ominous jealousies, and distrust. Djuradj Stratimirovich-Balsha, prince
of Zeta and son-in-law of Lazar, and some vojvodas of the
northern regions were delayed by local "revolts" and opposition. Historians are still trying to ascertain whether the
revolts were real or simply used as excuses. Two other of
Lazar's sons-in-law, according to national tradition and accepted by some historians, were bitterly divided, under the
influence of their wives. According to chroniclers, national
bards, and traditional Kosovo saga, Vuk Brankovich of the
old aristocracy, who married Mara, and Milosh Obilich, of
lesser birth, who married Vukosava, fell prey to the ongoing
feud between the two sisters. (Lazar's geneological history,
as presented by the historian Aleksa Ivich, however, does
not register Milosh Obilich among Lazar's sons-in-law.)

To make things worse, several well-known and gallant
Serbian and Bulgarian princes were at that time already in
the service of the Turkish conqueror, burdened by the obligations of vassalage. Among them, Dragash and Konstantin
ruled in the area between Serres and Kustendil, while the
sons of the late King Vukashin, Marko and Andrias, ruled
as vassals in the regions of today's western Macedonia. One
should keep in mind that at that time feudal mores required the vassal to serve his lord and not his people.

Prince Lazar could have taken some moral comfort from
the fact that he and his people were defenders of Christian
civilization, and that the forthcoming battle would probably be the last chance for Balkan Christians to repulse the
Moslems. Some historians will dispute it, but there are
others who maintain that quite a few among the leaders
in the neighboring states—from Bulgaria, the Danubian
lands, and even from the area of today's Croatia—took part
in the battle. It is indisputable, however, that among those
who joined the Serbs were some Albanian princes. Even
though no Albanian state had yet existed, Albanian tribes
were close allies of the Serbs, and friendly relations between

Serbian and Albanian chieftains were the natural result of their common desire to get rid of, first the Byzantine and then the Turkish oppressors. John Castriota (of Serbian origin), the father of the most prominent Albanian, Skanderbeg, came to Kosovo at the head of a combined Serbian-Albanian force mobilized in the area of Debar. Among auxiliary troops were the volunteers led by Palatine Nicolas Gara (Gorjanski), another one of Lazar's sons-in-law.

From the time that the Serbian notables and church dignitaries met in the city of Skopia (Skoplje), after the fatal battle in which King Vukashin and his army perished (Maritsa, 1371), and chose Lazar Hrebeljanovich as their leader, he enjoyed great popularity and respect. In addition to his personal qualities, he was also the husband of Militsa, the great granddaughter of Stefan Nemanja, the founder of the Nemanjich dynasty. He therefore had some hereditary right to the throne of Serbia. Wise, charitable, well-cultured, and skillful soldier, he defeated the Turks in encounters that took place in 1381 and 1386, but it was becoming ever more evident that Lazar was winning battles but losing the war.

Lazar's Bosnian ally, Tvrtko I, defeated the Turks when they probed Bosnian territory (1386 and 1388). All this, however, made the Turks only more resolute, and as the year 1389 came, they were ready. The Eastern Christians in the Balkans were now faced, not by scattered Turkish forces, but by a great army. Sultan Murad led his army straight toward Lazar's capital (Krushevats). There was a bloody Turkish assault on the fortress at Nish, which the Serbs defended heroically for twenty-five days. This is where Murad himself had an opportunity to evaluate the morale and effectiveness of the enemy. When Murad's scouts reported the concentration of a large Serbian army at Kosovo, he marched immediately to meet it. Thus the Balkan Christians and the Moslems were locked in a decisive battle, a battle that the Moslems saw as an opportunity to break the backbone of Serbian resistance.

According to Serbian bards and tradition, Murad sent the following message to Lazar: "Oh Lazar, thou head of the Serbians: There was not and never can be one land in the hands of two masters. . . . No more can two sultans rule here. . . . Come straight to meet me at Kosovo! The sword will decide for us."

Modern historians have had understandable difficulties in trying to decipher the realities of the battle of Kosovo. They have had to sift through a myriad of often rhapsodic and idealized, mostly apologetical, renditions of relevant decisions and events. Contemporary chroniclers, and later a whole lot of biographers and "history writers," as a rule had to keep in mind the interests of their protectors and sponsors, with objectivity not always their trademark. The casual author, for instance, thought nothing of reviving King Vukashin (eighteen years after his death) and to bring him to Kosovo as a participant, with "his thirty thousand troops." Groping through all this poetic license was unavoidable. But to the credit of epic writers, many of them provided data that were later corroborated by more reliable sources.

It is quite certain that Prince Lazar must have held some kind of war council with his vojvodas on the eve of the battle. Some among those present must have had apprehensions about Serbian prospects, especially in the light of the hesitancy, lukewarm enthusiasm, and even disloyalty among some Serbian warriors. Prince Lazar could easily have agreed with the evaluation which a national bard put into the mouth of Vuk Brankovich: "Fight we may, but conquer we cannot. . . ." Lazar could also have believed that some of his vojvodas were seriously thinking of passing over to the camp of the Sultan, among them Milosh Obilich, who was seen conferring with two other commanders and inquiring about Turkish battle deployment.

On the eve preceding the day of the battle, Prince Lazar, according to the Chronicles of Pech and Tronosha, and later the Chronicle of Monk Pahomie, asked for a golden

goblet of wine to be brought to him. In his toast he mentioned three brave and dashing vojvodas as possible traitors,
who were "thinking of deserting me and going over to the
Turkish side." These three were Ivan Kosanchich, Milan of
Toplitsa, and Milosh Obilich. Prince Lazar appealed to
Milosh not to betray him, and drank a toast to him: "Do
not be faithless, and take this golden cup from me as a
souvenir." Milosh responded with a few words of noble
indignation: "Oh Tsar, treachery now sits alongside your
knee," an allusion that Vuk Brankovich was responsible
for this lack of confidence. This scene on the eve of the
battle reminds one very much of the Christian saga of the
Last Supper, where Lazar emerges as a person similar to
Christ, knows very well the inevitability of treachery
among humans as well as knowing his own fate. Lazar behaved as a good Christian should, and had no rancor even
toward those who failed him. As for Milosh, he too behaved as a gallant Christian: "For thy goblet I thank you. For
thy speech, Tsar Lazar, I thank you not. . . . Tomorrow,
in the battle of Kosovo, I will perish fighting for the Christian faith."

It is indeed interesting that the Romanized West never
saw Lazar and Milosh, and their likes of Serbian Orthodoxy, as fighters for Christianity. It is well to recall, however, that before going into battle, Lazar left the Serbian
people the famous statement, which they have eternally
treasured and which is the essence of the Gospel Message:
"The earthly kingdom is short-lived, but the Heavenly One
is forever."

As for the Kosovo Battle, all available information seems
to confirm that Murad succeeded in surprising the Serbian
army, as he had done at Maritsa in 1371. In accordance
with the advice of his commander Evrenos Bey (of Greek
origin), he launched his attack early in the morning while
Lazar and his comrades were at prayers in the nearby
Samodrezha Church. It was there that news reached him
that the enemy was already attacking his front lines. It

was there, also, that he was informed that Milosh and his two Godbrothers, Ivan and Milan, had been seen riding out in the early dawn toward the Turkish lines. This must have strengthened his belief that the three Vojvodas were indeed traitors, and that Vuk Brankovich was right when he expressed doubts about Milosh. He must have thought of the summons he had sent to all Serbs before the battle, which according to national tradition reads: "Whoever born of Serbian blood or kin comes not to fight the Turks at Kosovo, to him never son or daughter born, no child to heir his land or bear his name. For him no grape grow red, no corn grow white, in his hand nothing prosper. May he live alone, unloved, and die unmourned, alone!"

As Lazar blessed his soldiers, he led them into battle, the clash that was to decide the fate of Balkan Eastern Orthodox nations for a long period to come. The Turkish historian Neshri describes the first phase of the battle in the following words:

> The archers of the faithful shot their arrows from both sides. Numerous Serbians stood as if they were mountains of iron. When the rain of arrows was a little too sharp for them, they began to move, and it seemed as if the waves of the Black Sea were making noise. . . . Suddenly the infidels stormed against the archers of the left wing, attacked them in the front, and, having divided their ranks, pushed them back. The infidels destroyed also the regiment. . . that stood behind the left wing. . . . Thus the Serbians pushed back the whole left wing, and when the confounding news of this disaster was spread among the Turks they became very low-spirited. . . . Bayazet, with the right wing, was as little moved as the mountain on the right of his position (Kopaonik). But he saw that very little was wanting to lose the Sultan's whole army.

But the quick thinking and decisiveness of the Sultan's son turned the flow of the battle. Among the Turks he was known as "Ildarin" (Lightning). He attacked the flank of the advancing Serbian force, and succeeded in repulsing and throwing into considerable disarray the hitherto victorious

Christians. At that critical moment, a Serbian corps of some 12,000 cuirassiers was withdrawn from the battle by their commander, Vuk Brankovich. He apparently either lost his nerve or thought it inadvisable to lose all of his men in a futile battle. But Lazar was of a different disposition. He was resolute to fight to the end, and the end soon came. He tried to rally his disheartened troops around him, and led them into a new attack, which failed. Inevitably, the morale of the Serbs plummeted. Wounded, Lazar was taken prisoner, and his army, rapidly falling apart, was beaten and dispersed on the early afternoon of that very day.

Serbian chroniclers maintain that, as he was led to Murad's tent, Lazar saw the wounded Vojvoda Milosh there, and only then realized what a heroic deed he had done. Deeply touched, Lazar gave Milosh his blessing, as he realized that Milosh had mortally wounded the Sultan, striking him in the abdomen with a concealed dagger. Milosh got access to Murad's tent by pretending he had come to surrender and wanted to kiss the Sultan's foot.

There they were, in that tent, all the featured actors of the Kosovo drama, ready for the final Shakesperian resolution of the plot. One of Murad's close advisers (Ali Pasha) lay dead already; he too a victim of Milosh's dagger. Prince Bayazet ordered Lazar and his nobles executed by the sword, in the presence of the dying Sultan. The Serbian nobles asked to be beheaded first. Bayazet turned down their plea. But when one of Lazar's vojvodas, Krajimir of Toplista, asked for permission to hold his own robe so that Lazar's head would not fall to the bare ground, Bayazet, impressed by such loyalty, granted the request. Milosh Obilich was beheaded first. As Lazar started to say a few last words to his nobles, he was abruptly stopped by the Turks. Kneeling, he could only utter: "My God, receive my soul."

Murad lived long enough to see his enemies beheaded. As he died, his younger son Bayazet made sure immediately

to eliminate his brother Jacub, who had also taken part in
the battle, and thus assure his ascendance to the highest
position as head of the victorious Turks. Moreover, he took
Lazar's daughter Olivera into his harem, and led the Turks
in other battles. The Serbian princess must have meant a
lot to the Turk called Lightning, because when thirteen
years later he was taken prisoner by the leader of the
Tartars (Tamerlane), Bayazet chose poison rather than
watch the jewel of his harem, Olivera, serve her new
master.

As Vidovdan 1389 came to a close, and the sun went
down behind the mountains of Zeta (Montenegro) in the
west the night that would last five centuries began. Two
tsars, both in their sixties, lay dead on the plain of Kosovo,
surrounded by their slain brave warriors. Murad's body was
carried by his warriors all the way to Asia Minor, to the
city of Broussa. Present at the burial ceremony were two
Serbian Vojvodas, the ones that were ordered by Bayazet
to escort the body of their enemy. Today, the visiting
tourist is told that the two sarcophaguses, next to Murad's
contain the "bodies of unknown decapitated Serbian
nobles."

By the grace of the new Turkish Sultan, the Serbs were
allowed to pick up the severed head of their leader, and
carry it together with the body to the Church of Vazne-
senje Hristovo in Prishtina. Later the remains were moved
to the Monastery Ravanitsa, which Lazar had built. The
Serbian Church proclaimed Prince Lazar a saint and holy
martyr. The mutilated body of the Saint Prince could not
however, rest long in his native land. As the Turks moved
to the north, his remains were carried to Frushka Gora
(Vrdnik Monastery) in Srem, at that time in Hungary. The
wandering bones had to be moved a fourth time, when in
1941 the Croatian Ustashi began pillaging Serbian holy
places in the newly created Axis satellite, Independent
State of Croatia. Tsar Lazar's relics were taken to Belgrade
and now rest in front of the altar of the main Orthodox

Cathedral. New generations can view and honor Lazar's shrunken body in the robe of faded red and gold brocade, a dark cloth hiding his head and the gap between it and his shoulders.

For the Serbs, Kosovo became a symbol of steadfast courage and sacrifice for honor, much as the Alamo for Americans—only Kosovo was the Alamo writ large, where Serbs lost their whole nation, but in the words of Sam Houston, it would be "remembered" and avenged.

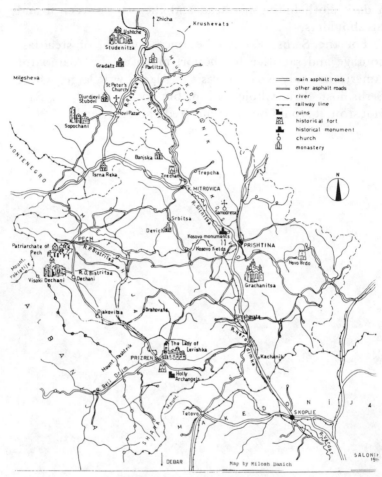

Kosovo: Churches and Monasteries

# CHAPTER III

## RASCIA (RASHKA) AND KOSOVO MONUMENTS

If one were to visit the territories of former Rascia (Rashka) and Kosovo, one would encounter many visible landmarks that are witnesses to Serbia's medieval grandeur. An extensive discussion of these art monuments is beyond the scope of this study. Rather, in this brief chapter we wish to examine some of the surviving monuments as documents of Serbia's cultural legacy in Kosovo and adjoining areas. It is our hope that the following text, supported with illustrations, will raise the reader's awareness of the importance of that artistic heritage.

Serbia's (Rashka's) opportunity to announce its cultural presence in the Byzantine-dominated Balkans came with Serbia's methodical consolidation of her rise as a political power under a single and powerful leader. This evolution in Serbia's medieval history was particularly marked in the latter half of the 12th century, when the Latin West, led by the Venetians, struck against Byzantium during ·the fourth Crusade, and finally sacked Constantinople in 1204. Serbia was thus presented with an opportunity to advance its own political and religious cause, due in no small part to the divisions within the Byzantine empire, divisions that lasted until the restoration of the empire in 1261 under the Palaeologan dynasty.

Nemanja, the founder of Serbian medieval statehood, deserves the credit for not missing the opportunity to advance the Serbian cause politically, and his son Sava for expanding Serbia in the realm of culture and art. Nemanja was certainly aware of the need for a strong Serbian political unit that required cultural manifestations that could easily be identified with the Serbian people. The choice of Sava to implement these political and cultural plans was not accidential. As a politically astute leader, Nemanja knew that the great centers of Constantinople and Thessalonika in the East, and his own Zeta littoral in the west were culturally rich but stylistically diverse regions. Byzantium abounded in artists of every kind, while the coast of Zeta provided stone masons of unparalleled skills. But it was only under the generous patronage of the members of the Nemanjich dynasty, and above all under the sage and brilliant guidance of Sava, that these two different artistic spirits could be united to produce from old tradition-bound forms new and creative combinations that can easily be identified as the art style of Rashka.

Sava, a Mont Athos monk, scholar, and theologian (graduate of Hilandar Monastery), was eminently prepared to build the foundations upon which a national culture would grow within the religious environment of Eastern Orthodoxy. As a man of his time, a diplomat above all, serving his newly-born state, he had the opportunity to know most of the leading figures of the era: from emperors sitting on the various thrones of segmented Byzantium, to the heads of churches and spiritual leaders of monastic communities, from Nicea and Jerusalem to the shores of the Adriatic and beyond. In his travels he became acquainted with architecture and religous art in churches and monasteries throughout Byzantium and all the way to the Holy Land.

Sava learned from the treasured stores of knowledge safeguarded in monastic libraries. He must have known personally many of his contemporary learned authors and theologians, either as friends or adversaries. He was able to commission from Constantinople some of the most out-standing painters of that period. Never again in its history would Serbia have a son of his stature and impact. He was the youngest member of the family, whose father was to follow in his footsteps as a monk, and whose ruling brot-hers would listen to and heed his advice.

Abroad, the Byzantines hated him (the Greek archbis-hop of neighboring Ohrid anathematized him when he succeeded in gaining autocephaly for the Serbian Church), but still needed him. The Bulgarians revered him, while the Papal Alliance avoided dealings with him. When the Byzan-tines and the Latins were dividing the Balkans, Sava made sure that the dividing line did not go through Rascia. He was determined to withstand Catholic religious pressures, and to establish Orthodoxy as a national faith, and through translated liturgical services to give it a Serbian cast.

These unique geo-political circumstances had a char-acteristic impact upon the evolving Serbian cultural mani-festations, the surviving remains of which can readily be seen not only in the former lands of Rashka and Kosovo, but even beyond. Nemanja, who did not want to be re-membered by castles or fortresses but by churches, and Sava proved to be a magnificent combination: a pragmatic father to construct a viable frame and a sophisticated and artistically sensitive son to fill it with relevant content. Above all, Nemanja and Sava set a precedent to be follow-ed by the other members of the Nemanjich dynasty, their noblemen, and high clergy—the end result being untold artistic and cultural riches, the pride of the Serbian nation to this day.

One of the early structures sponsored by Nemanja was dedicated to a military saint, Saint George, and placed as a proud symbol on a tall promontory overlooking Nemanja's capital city of Ras. It was a single nave domed structure, and its twin-towered entrance gave it the popular name, *Djurdjevi Stubovi* (1170-1171). This church was sumptuously decorated (1175) by an outstanding but anonymous artist. Due to military and other calamities, the frescoes survived only in small fragments (recently the structure was restored and roofed). In spite of the losses of painted surfaces, the entire iconographic schema is clear: a lower zone of standing saints; two zones of compositions from the life of Christ; and in the dome the image of the Lord in bust.

An addition to the painted program of Djurdjevi Stubovi was provided by Nemanja's great grandson, King Dragutin in 1282-1283. Most interesting for Serbian history is the painted program of the groundfloor chapel, under the entrance tower, created as a burial place for Dragutin himself. Here one sees the members of the Nemanjich dynasty, from founder onward (with their wives) in ceremonial procession approaching the Enthroned Christ. In the groin vault covering this chapel one sees as a permanent document for posterity, four illustrated events: Nemanja as Monk Simeun reliquishing his throne in favor of his son Stefan; the enthronement of Urosh I as King of Serbia; Dragutin's assumption of the throne; and finally, his relinquishing the throne in favor of his brother Milutin.

Nemanja's laying of religious foundations was more than an artistic endeavor. It served political and religious purposes, but it was above all aimed at the salvation of his soul. To house his own crypt, Nemanja built a monastery (1183-1191), well-hidden in the canyon of a swift tributary of the Ibar river, to which he gave the name *Studenitsa*. It is to this site that Nemanja withdrew from ruling duties to become Monk Simeun, living there for over a year and a half before going to Mount Athos. Remote in the mountains, Studenitsa's location is beautifully and vividly described by Sava in his biography of Nemanja: "This place was a barren hunting range teeming with wild beasts. When

Djurdjevi Stubovi, Church of St George, partial restoration
(photo: Joanne A. Rathman)

Zhicha Monastery, Church of the Savior
(photo: Joanne A. Rathman)

Studenitsa Monastery, Church of the Virgin
(photo: Ljubica D. Popovich)

Studenitsa Monastery, view of frescoes
(photo: Joanne A. Rathman)

Milesheva Monastery, Church of the Ascension
(photo: Ljubica D. Popovich)

Milesheva Monastery: View of "White Angel"

Pech Patriarchate
(photo: Laurie C. Simpson)

Monastery Banjska, Church of Saint Stefan
(photo: Momchilo Djordjevich)

Sopochani Monastery, Church of the Trinity
(photo: Ljubica D. Popovich)

Grachanitsa Monastery, Church of the Annunciation
(photo: Ljubica D. Popovich)

Cathedral of the Virgin Ljevishka (Prizren)
(photo: Ljubica D. Popovich)

Dechani Monastery
(photo: unknown)

he came to hunt, our Master and Autocrat Stefan Nemanja, who ruled over all Serbian lands, felt a desire to build
on this deserted spot a monastery of his own."

The Church of the Virgin, the center of this monastic
complex, later served as a prototype for several other
churches destined to be burial places of Serbian kings.
While the frescoes in the church are characteristically
Byzantine, the marble portals and their sculptures and re-
liefs typically Romanesque, the parts taken together bear
the imprint of the Serbian spirit. After the transfer of
Nemanja's remains from Mount Athos to Studenitsa,
Byzantine painters were brought in to decorate the walls
of the church (1209). Most likely, Sava helped plan the
iconographic program, and most certainly gave instructions
about the historical personages to be included. Although
the painter left an inscription in Greek at the base of the
dome (now only partially preserved), all other inscriptions
throughout the church are in Serbian, written in large and
beautifully formalized letters, undoubtedly under the explicit influence of Sava or perhaps by his own hand.

To the original church a large outer narthex was added
in 1235. Here, too, fragments of fresco paintings are preserved. Among the more significant ones are those in the
south chapel, where one finds the oldest preserved historical compositions with specifically Serbian subjects, which
together with the religious scenes indicate that they were
inspired directly by Sava's writing. The historical events
deal with the transfer of Simeun's relics from Mount Athos
to Studenitsa. Also present are the dynastic portraits, from
the founder to King Radoslav carrying the model, indicat-
ing that he was the donor of this addition to the Church of
the Virgin.

To the south stands a much smaller structure, the so-
called King's Church, built by Nemanja's great grandson
King Stefan Milutin. This powerful and wealthy ruler of
Serbia for almost forty years reputedly built or renovated
a church for each year of his reign. Some say that this

number is exaggerated, but the numerous religious structures still standing throughout Serbian lands, and even reaching to Jerusalem and Constantinople, are historical testimony to King Milutin's generosity.

The King's Church, small, single naved, and domed, was decorated in or around the year 1314. The total iconographic program is relatively well preserved. In the opinion of scholars, the quality of the preserved frescoes is the best of this period outside Constantinople. Besides representations of the twelve liturgical feasts, saints and prophets, and cycles from the life of Christ, there are dynastic portraits from Nemanja and Sava to King Milutin (holding a model of the chapel) and his child queen, Byzantine Palaeologan Princess Simonis. Although this tiny monument endured much destruction over the centuries, a part of the king's inscription remains and reads: ". . . whoever alters this let him be cursed by God and sinful me, amen." The long dead king still seems to be guarding the small foundation.

Following the example of the founder of the dynasty, the sons, grandsons, and other descendents continued building churches throughout Serbian-held lands. All of these structures, with their plans, elevations, and artistic embellishments, are grouped together into a stylistic unit known as the Rashka School, being distinctly different from other Serbian schools, such as the Morava School to the east and the Zeta School to the west.

Rashka and Kosovo were at that time a single political and cultural entity. As all things in medieval society, churches had their hierarchical order. Famous and venerated as it was, the Studenitsa Monastery was not the first-ranked church among Serbian-built religious structures, since it was not planned as the See of a Serbian archbishop.

The Church of the Ascension of Christ in the *Zhicha Monastery*, built by Sava and his brother Stefan (after 1207), was perceived as the "Mother of Serbian Churches," and eventually became the coronation church of Serbian kings, beginning with Stefan the First-Crowned. As mentioned by Sava's biographer, Theodosius, Sava brought with him the builders and marble workers "from the Greek land." For the painted decoration of this church, executed about 1220, Sava brought painters directly from Constantinople.

It is surprising that Sava, who took care of the planning and execution of so many of the early Nemanja structures, did not build his own resting place. Nemanja's grandson, King Vladislav, buried Sava in the famous church of the Ascension of Christ in his own *Milesheva Monastery*. This domed building of the Rashka style was erected near Prijepolje probably just before the year 1230. At that time it was decorated with frescoes, whose artists tried to emulate the noted Byzantine mosaic technique. From this church comes some of the most beautifully painted images that have been preserved in the entire corpus of Serbian medieval paintings. Among them is the elegant and serene figure of the Virgin from the Annunciation.

In 1236, King Vladislav brought the body of his venerated uncle to this church. Sava died in Trnovo (Bulgaria) a year earlier, while on yet another diplomatic mission, this time successfully to negotiate authocephalic status for the sisterly Bulgarian Orthodox Church. It was a difficult task for the Serbian king to bring Sava's body to his native land. Sava was so venerated in Bulgaria that Vladislav's father-in-law, the "fearless" Tsar Asen II, lacked the courage to let Sava's earthly remains be taken out of the country, fearing the rage of the local population. Some popular tradition has it that Vladislav literally stole the body of his uncle and brought it to Milesheva. Actually he had permission from the Tsar, but to avoid possible incidents the body was removed secretly. Some years later, Vladislav was also buried there.

The tomb of Sava, the first Serbian archbishop, became one of the venerated places for the Serbs. Even after his death, he had a special role in the life of his nation and its rulers. In the fourteenth century, Bosnian King Tvrtko I crowned himself King of Serbia on Sava's grave, an act obviously full of significance. Another nobleman, Stjepan Vukchich, assumed on the tomb of Sava the title of "Herceg [heir] of Saint Sava."

The Turks burned Milesheva in 1459, but the church building survived. Some 150 years later, the Islamized Albanian from Prizren, Grand Vizier Sinnan Pasha, campaigning in Hungary and dissatisfied with the behavior of Serbian homesteaders, ordered Sava's body disinterred and burned on a pyre in the Vrachar area of Belgrade. The Serbian Orthodox Church declared this youngest son of Nemanja a national saint.

In the period between 1544-1557, the Milesheva Monastery became a "publishing house," printing on its own presses numerous liturgical books. The popularity of these among the Slavs was considerable, and some reached as far as Russia. In return, some gifts were sent from Russia to the monastery. For example, still preserved in the monastic treasury is a chalice donated by Tsar Ivan the Terrible in 1558.

Milesheva had its own school where Serbian children learned to read. Among the pupils was a youngster later taken by the Turks into the Janissary corps, the renowned Mehmed Pasha Sokolovich, who subsequently rose to the rank of Grand Vizier in Constantinople.

Twice more, in 1689 and 1782, the Turks set fire to the monastery. Its turbulent history has left its scars especially strongly on the fresco surfaces. Yet, it has one of the most beautiful and moving frescoes of Serbian medieval art, a detail of a larger composition, the "White Angel," still resplendant in its majestic presence.

Another Serbian monastery, *Sopochani,* was chosen by King Stefan Urosh I as the site of his final resting place. Hidden among the gently rolling hills in the heartland of Serbia of the Nemanjich dynasty, it lies near the ancient

capital of Ras and the source of the river Rashka. Its horizon is dominated by the abovementioned Djurdjevi Stubovi. In some ways it matched its founder's nature, a dif-
fident and demure king, rather spartan in life philosophy
and thoroughly unglamorous. Dedicated to the Trinity,
Sopochani was built about the year 1265. Soon after its
construction, King Urosh brought the body of his father,
Stefan the First-Crowned, to be buried there. Subsequently, when King Urosh died in exile in Hum, his body was
brought to Sopochani. Also interred there is King Urosh's
mother, Anna Dandolo, the grand daughter of Enrico
Dandolo, the Doge of Venice. The death of this Serbian
queen is one of the most important historical compositions preserved on the walls of Serbian medieval churches.

Architecturally, Sopochani follows the tradition of the
Rashka school, but the chapels used for burials make it appear as a standard three-nave basilica. Sopochani suffered
greatly from natural and war disasters, partially destroyed
but never diminishing the beauty of its fresco decoration.
Scholars are still debating the origin of Sopochani's master
painters. Among them was one great but anonymous artist
who painted the central areas under the dome, as well as
some of the standing figures. His brilliant work was one of
the greatest in all of Europe at that time.

As in Milesheva, the walls are painted in yellow, with
coverings in gold leaf (now long lost) in order to emulate
the mosaic technique. All of the inscriptions are in Serbian,
and some of the faces of the Serbian archbishops (painted
in liturgical procession in the apse) convey a feeling of the
presence of living persons. Besides the religious compositions, there are numerous representations of scenes related
to the Nemanjich dynasty. Many portraits of Serbian kings
and their queens and princes, are seen under a benevolent
image of the blessing Christ.

Earlier we mentioned King Milutin's generosity in the
building of churches and monasteries. If space permitted,
we would discuss a number of other churches built or

restored by him. One especially deserves mention, the renovated cathedral church of Prizren, the *Virgin Ljevishka* (1307). Its brilliantly painted frescoes by a group of artists who worked in Ohrid (Michael, Euthychios, and Astrapa) still fascinate the observer in spite of the damage inflicted by the Moslems when they converted the church into a mosque. Among the religious compositions and the individual images of various male and female saints, one can also see the members of the Nemanjich dynasty, from the founder in his monastic robes to the princes who went to serve the church and the nation in religious capacities, to the richly garbed King Milutin, in his splendor rivaling the Byzantine emperor himself.

In the vicinity of Kosovska Mitrovitsa, between 1313 and 1317, King Milutin renovated an older church, *Banjska* and dedicated it to Saint Stefan, the namesake of the founder of the Serbian dynasty and many other Serbian kings. This structure also belongs to the Rashka school and was once richly decorated by sculptural carvings. Its frescoes, however, are totally lost, and the church was greatly damaged when the Turks turned it into a mosque. Nevertheless, the beauty of its polychromatic walls still testifies to the past splendor of the church, which was originally planned as King Milutin's final resting place. His royal ring is still preserved, bearing the inscription: "God help him who wears it . . . . "

The last church built by King Milutin—*Grachanitsa*—is certainly second to none among the Serbian masterpieces. Built on Kosovo Field between 1317-1321, it was the See of the bishop of Lipljan, and ultimately it might have been planned as the final resting place of King Milutin. It is architecturally different from the previously discussed Rashka school of architecture. Its master builders did not have a Romanesque stylistic orientation; rather they turned to Byzantine architecture as the source of inspiration.

The church itself is a cross-in-square plan, preceded by an open narthex, and surmounted not by one, but by five domes: the central being the largest and the four corner ones being much smaller. The exterior walls show the so-called cloisonne technique, in which stone blocks are enclosed by bricks set into the thick mortar beds. Impressive are the soaring heights of the church, and the mysteriously lit complex interior spaces, still covered in their entirety by an almost intact fresco ensemble.

Among the standing saints and Christological compositions, are the scenes of the Last Judgment (covering the entire west wall) and the portraits of King Milutin and his Byzantine-born Queen Simonis, daughter of Emperor Andronikos II. The aged king and his still young queen, splendidly dressed in their bejeweled garments, are given the crown by an angel, the messenger of God. As in the case of many paintings of saints, the eyes of Queen Simonis are dug out. This event was much later immortalized in a poem by Serbian poet and diplomat Milan Rakich, which reads in part:

> Oh, pretty image, an Albanian has dug out your eyes,
> With a knife when no one would see him.

and

> But I can see, oh woeful Simonis, your long dug out
> Eyes, still gleaming at me from the wall.

The names of the Grachanitsa painters are not known. It is a well-established fact, however, that King Milutin maintained a group of artists, whose works scholars call the Court School of King Milutin. As mentioned above, the names of some of them are known, and they came from Ohrid to work for the Serbian king. Some of these painters left their signatures on their works, thus immortalizing themselves and their royal sponsor. In the sponsorship of artists, Milutin followed the tradition of his family. His mother, Queen Jelena, supported the school for embroidery arts, and undoubtedly many a Serbian woman honed her skills there. Moreover, Milutin's brother, King Dragutin, also sponsored an art school specializing in applied arts and crafts.

Art historians in general, and Byzantologists in particular, have written volumes dealing with the style and iconography of Serbian frescoes. In general, they agree that Serbian paintings preserved on the walls of these medieval churches constitute a continuity in Byzantine artistic expression during the period when the artistic production of Constantinople was severely curtailed due to the political situation of the empire in the late 12th and early 13th centuries. Most scholars also agree that Serbian art served as a link between the East and West, transmitting to Western artists, eager to learn and experiment, the venerable old tradition kept alive in the superior Byzantine technique of frescoes and mosaics, as well as style. This was the period of the 13th and 14th centuries, when Byzantium was undergoing an artistic revival (after 1261), and just as the West was on the threshold of the classical revival, self-discovery, and the renaissance.

The center of Serbian Orthodox Christendom was the monastic complex at Pech, most often referred to as the *Patriarchate.* Located in the vicinity of the rugged Rugovo pass, a nightmare to any intruder, the walled monastery conveys a feeling of remoteness, in a physical and spiritual sense. The need to hide was understandable in view of the fact that Zhicha, exposed in the plains, was sacked on several occasions by the maurading Bulgarians, Mongols, and other passing invaders. Also, as the See, first of Serbian archbishops and later of Serbian patriarchs for three centuries, the monastery required seclusion. Many church dignitaries are buried there.

The complex itself consists of several churches, chapels, and a large outer narthex, all attached and forming an inseparable unit. The oldest is the church of the *Holy Apostles,* built by Archbishop Arsenije in the period between 1235-1250. Some of the original frescoes are still preserved. Especially noteworthy is the majestic representation in the dome of the Ascension of Christ. To the north, Archbishop Nikodimus added the church of *Saint Demetrios* during the years 1316-1324. The fresco ensemble is almost completely preserved. The images are signed in Serbian, while the painter left a signature in Greek in the apse of the church. To the south, the famous Serbian Archbishop, writer, and architect, Danilo II, in 1330 added the church dedicated to the Virgin. Among its preserved frescoes are portraits of Archbishop Danilo with a model of the church, and his namesake, the prophet Daniel.

There are other Serbian monasteries and churches (preserved or in ruins) that dot the landscape of Kosovo. Among these are Devich, Gorioch, and Lipljan. Some of these served as sources of inspiration to national bards composing verses of epic poetry, e.g. Samodrezha near Prishtina, one of King Milutin's capitals.

Probably the most important of medieval Serbia's Kosovo cities was Prizren, Tsar Dushan's capital. In its vicinity Dushan provided for his final resting place, the only structure that he had an opportunity to build as donor. The church was dedicated to the *Holy Archangels*. Erected between 1347 and 1352, it was one of the most magnificent of Serbian medieval royal foundations. Its grandeur was meant to match in every way Dushan's ambitions, particularly his planned conquest of Byzantium. The young Tsar ordered the annual production of his silver mine at Novo Brdo to be set aside to cover the expenses of building and decorating his ambitious enterprise.

Although chronically late, the style chosen was the Rashka school. The exterior was purple and yellow marble blocks, while red stone was carefully selected for the interior. All of these colors had royal connotations. No expense was spared on the interior, resplendent in marble incrustations, goldleaf in vaults, silver stars, and lavish mosaics. A magnificent mosaic floor was in the process of execution when Dushan's sudden death resulted in bringing his body for burial there.

When the conquering Turks came to the region in 1455, this beautiful structure was almost completely destroyed. The conquerors ordered the building razed, and the marble blocks reused for Sinnan Pasha's mosque. The excavations between the two world wars, and after World War II, yielded a few precious fragments which attest to the church's past splendor, and some of the large foundation stones remain. In the post-World War II period, Tsar Dushan's remains were brought to Belgrade to rest in Saint Mark's church, built in the interwar period as a large replica of Grachanitsa.

Besides the cathedral church, Virgin of Levishka, and the ruins of Dushan's church, the Serbian royal city of Prizren still guards several national treasures, such as the churches of Saint Nikola, Saint Mark, and the Savior, dating from the 14th century, as well as a 13th century painted cave-hermitage church of Peter Korishki.

No enumeration of Serbian monasteries in Kosovo and vicinity would be complete without mentioning the majesty and serenity of the largest of all Serbian medieval churches, the *Dechani Monastery*. It was built for King Stefan Urosh III (Dechanski) between 1327 and 1335, and dedicated to the Savior. Its immense painted decoration was completed under Tsar Dushan about 1345-1350. This church, too, follows the tradition of the Rashka style, although there are some elements of the Gothic. The chief architect was a Franciscan from the Serbian royal city of Kotor, Fra Vita, who signed his name on one of the stone lintels. The names of the assistants are also known, the brothers Djordje, Dobroslav, and Nikola, all trained in the Kotor school. The naos frescoes were finished about 1435, the narthex only about 1450. Dechani contains more than a thousand compositions, with an estimated 10,000 painted figures. There are more than twenty biblical cycles on the walls, from Genesis to the Last Judgment. This is certainly the largest surviving iconographic complex ever created within the Byzantine sphere of influence. There are royal portraits, and an immense genealogical tree of the Nemanjich dynasty. What these frescoes lack in artistic qualities they make up in quantities.

Tradition says that the widow of Kosovo martyr Prince Lazar, Princess Militsa, gave the monastery a giant candle to be lit only when the Kosovo defeat of 1389 was avenged. In 1913, at the conclusion of the victories in the Balkan wars, King Petar Karadjordjevich I lit that candle, signifying the liberation of Kosovo (Rebecca West, *Black Lamb and Grey Falcon: A Journey through Yugoslavia;* New York, 1982, p. 985). An eyewitness insists that King Alexander Karadjordjevich lit two candles on August 19, 1924. The body of the founder, King Stefan Dechanski, who is considered a martyr among Serbs is still resting in his church.

All of these churches and monastic establishments, the religious and artistic shrines of the Kosovo region, offer obvious testimony that Kosovo was one of the ethnically strongest Serbian territories in medieval times. The foundation charters of these monasteries are among the most reliable primary sources about the population of that period, comparable to contemporary census documents. The Dechani charter, for example, lists 2,166 agricultural homesteads and 266 stock-raising properties that were deeded to the monastery. Only 44 among them can be identified as ethnically Albanian. Finally, in contrast to all of the Serbian historical monuments in Kosovo, there is not a single Albanian one.

During the subsequent centuries, however, the ethnic picture changed dramatically. The scenes from Serbian history and the dynastic portraits of Serbian kings painted on the walls of these churches endured the passage of time. The population which venerated them did not fare so well, thinned out by wars and other misfortunes. With these circumstances in mind, it seems appropriate to ask, could Kosovo live without a strong Serbian presence in the area? Could Kosovo continue to be immortalized through the passage of centuries only by these religious shrines and the works of art? Isolated from the people for whom they were created, are they nothing but vulnerable stones? How did it all happen? Where did the Serbs go? Who brough the Albanians into Kosovo? The authors hope to give at least some partial answers to these questions in the chapters that follow.

# CHAPTER IV

## SERBS AND ALBANIANS UNDER TURKISH RULE

The end of the Serbian Despotate in 1459 was followed by the demise of the Kingdom of Bosnia (1463). The Ottoman Empire now ruled not only over all Serbs (except those in Montenegro of which more will be said later), but stretched all the way from Mesopotamia to the Danube, and westward to the Adriatic. Serbs, Greeks, Bulgars, and Albanians were subjugated, and they had no idea how long their plight would last. At the same time, some among them concluded that life would be easier if they converted to Islam. Many others decided to move out—to Hungary or to head for the coast and to look for a haven in Venice or in Venetian held territories in Dalmatia, or to try the gates of Dubrovnik, which in exchange for tribute to the Sultan, was allowed to retain its small territory free of Turks. Those who stayed and did not convert had one thing in common: all of them were classified as "giaurs," a category that lumped together all those who were not Moslems.

To the Turks the Byzantine and Roman faiths were two sides of the same coin, a logical conclusion. In real life, however, the best proof that it was not so, was to be found in the very fact of Turkish victory. It took them less than a century to annihilate three Balkan tsardoms, divided and never assisted by Christian Western Europe.

On the other hand, Christianity was the only single bond that the subjugated peoples of the Balkans now had in common. What else was there to hold on to until the Islamic flood should recede? Moreover, the Balkan peninsula became a two-realm society: Moslem and Christian, one privileged and the other discriminated against. It was up to the individual to decide whether he wanted to live and die as an exploited person, or the favored one. It was obvious that hard decisions had to be made.

The Turkish occupation did not mean the same thing for all Balkan nationalities. The Greeks, for example, who had played such an important role in the Byzantine world, were viewed with the greatest respect by the invader. The Turks were good fighters and eager to participate in the spoils of war, but when it came to bureaucracy and administration in general they were sadly lacking. It was not long after the fall of Constantinople that the city's Greek, Venetian, and Jewish communities began to bustle with activity and oppulence. Someone had to provide the continuity in commerce, administration, and in understanding the Balkan mosaic. By all standards, in the reality of the period, the Greeks had to be the ones.

When it came to choosing who would represent the Christians, and to provide spiritual leadership, the choice again fell to the Greeks. Having a Greek as Eastern Orthodox Patriarch in Constantinople made a substantial difference.

For the Serbs, a glimpse into the gruesomeness of their reality in that period is given us by a contemporary Serbian, turned adventurer, soldier of fortune, and author— Konstantin Mihailovich of Ostrovitsa. Serving for ten full years as a member of Turkish shock troops and fighting for Sultan Mehmed II, he later escaped to Hungary. Toward the end of his life, this gifted man wrote *Memoirs of a Janissary*, in the form of a general history of the Turks of his time. One of the events he described was the fall of the Serbian mining town of Novo Brdo into the hands of the Sultan. First, the Sultan ordered all gates closed except one, through which all of the inhabitants had to pass, leaving their possessions behind. "So they began passing through, one by one," writes Mihailovich, "and the Sultan, standing at the gate, was separating males from females . . . then he ordered the leaders beheaded. He saved 320 young men and 704 young women. . . . He distributed the women among his warriors, and the young men he took into the Janissary corps, sent them to Anatolia. . . . I was there, in that city of Novo Brdo, I who write this. . . ."

The shipping of young Christian men (and boys) to Turkish schools to become Janissaries, or if talented, to be a part of the administrative apparatus, was common practice in the Ottoman Empire. It was part of the tribute the Christian "rayah" had to pay to the Turks, but it was not always the same in all regions. It is not clear whether it was a compliment or a punishment when the Turks took more male children from one area than from another. Serbs were trying to hide their boys, only to realize later that the ones who were taken away fared much better in life.

Because religion, not nationality, was the fundamental factor in the Turkish concept of governing, it was possible for a "rayah" child to become a Grand Vizier of the Turkish Sultan. Mehmed Sokolovich, a Serbian child from a village near Vishegrad, was a Turkish Grand Vizier. He built that famous bridge on the river Drina, the subject of the book by Serbian Nobel Laureate, Ivo Andrich. In general, it can be said that compared to today's totalitarian societies, where party and creed adherence is a must, Turkish rulers come out rather liberal. As long as one was a devout Moslem, that was enough for the Sultan to expect allegiance. And allegiance he got. Mehmed Sokolovich served three of them in a row with the highest possible loyalty and fidelity.

As the Islamization process was taking place, it took
root better in some areas, among certain classes, and in
certain environments. For example, the process was much
faster in Albanian and Bosnian areas than in Serbia's former
state area. Accepting Islam in Albanian regions was a less
painful process, because the Albanians did not have an
autocephalous church, and their Christianity, whether
Latin or Byzantine, was a foreign product, either Greek
or Italian. And in Bosnia the widely spread Bogumil sect
did not hold Christianity in high esteem.

Wealth and material position were also important factors
that entered into the decision process at times of conversion. Town dwellers, land owners, and military oriented
personalities had to think in terms of Islam, if they wanted
to preserve what they had, and to take part in new accumu-
lation. Those with professional skills—artisans, doctors,
scholars, and administrators—could not expect to fare well
if they stuck to their old faith. This, however, was not true
of the common people and the peasants.

All of this played a role in defining the new stratifica-
tion of the society under Ottoman rule, as well as the
power balance among national groups. Undoubtedly, the
balance was shifting, and as far as the Albanians and Serbs
were concerned, it was shifting drastically in favor of the
Albanians, to the detriment of good relations between
them. With over thirty Grand Viziers of Albanian descent
during Ottoman rule, the top policy making machine was
indeed saturated with people of Albanian stock.

No one knew the effect of the nationality stock better
than the Dubrovnik colony of merchants in Constantinople.
Never did they have it better than when Sokolovich was
the Grand Vizier. Never were they hated and envied more
in Constantinople than when Djivo Djurdjevich and Pavle
Sorkochevich, the two senators from the city republic,
could come, just as many other Slavs of rank, and ask for
an audience and be received by the Grand Vizier with sym-
pathy and understanding. The Serbian historian, Radovan

Samardzich, describes it almost poetically in his book on Sokolovich:

> Sokolovich took great pleasure in talking with Dubrovchani because he could talk with them in his mother tongue, without witless, muddle-headed, and dangerous interpreters, obtaining firsthand detailed, and exact evaluations of conditions in Europe. . . . More than that, he experienced a personal satisfaction, impregnated with unspecified melancholy, on hearing in his own language all those expressions, thoughts, and cut-outs of life, which to his own Turks, even if they still knew the language, were becoming foreign. . . and when occasionally he would, with jestering sarcasm, frolic upon their poltroonery, easily detectable slyness, and clumsily hidden egoism, he [still] never. . . let them return to their quarters unhappy or discouraged.

One could contend that in this particular case the prominent Serbian historian had fallen prey to unscientific sentimentality, but there is no doubt that as far as the process of Islamization was concerned, Albanians in general showed themselves much more pliable than Serbs. The weight of their Albanian traditional load must have been a lighter burden. Theirs is the famous saying: "Ku ëste shpata ëste feja" (your faith is where the sword is). First class warriors, fascinated by guns, used to discipline and obeying when ruled by a strong hand, the Albanians represented a much better medium to be cast into the Turkish mold than the individualistic and unpredictable Serbs.

In the Turkish society which had several centuries to go before being seriously challenged, this was a crucial distinction that would decide the potential for advancement. After the Serbian Patriarchate was abolished (1556), it was a blessing for the Serbs to have had Mehmed Sokolovich in a position of power, who reopened the Patriarchate (1557) and placed his brother, Makarius, in charge. But the Serbs badly needed another Mehmed in 1776, when the Patriarchate was once again abolished. Unfortunately for them, one or two Serbian candles, at best, were not enough in five centuries of Turkish darkness. There is no doubt that the Albanians' continued presence at the seat of power gave them an upper hand, which was the beginning of a tragic divisiveness, of separate roads for them and for the Serbs. The former became the rulers and the latter the ruled.

This split, or a parting of the ways, is probably best seen in the gradual deterioration of relations between neighboring Montenegrin and Albanian tribes. In the early stages of Turkish occupation these relations were friendly. Living under similar conditions in the isolated highlands, having similar life patterns, traditions, and history, they were a world apart from the rest of the Balkans. They populated the roadless mountain areas that invaders had no particular desire to visit as long as their control was acknowledged by regular tax contributions and tributes. Usually they were left alone to lead and organize their own lives around their own social patterns. Their elected local leaders, together with their priests, ruled in strict observance of their traditions and customs. The Turkish judiciary never bothered the Christians unless Moslem rule or people were involved. In their relationships members of the two societies, Christian and Moslem (Montenegrin and Albanian, although sometimes not necessarily so clearly delineated), were generally cordial. Through common experiences and alliances in local conflicts, as well as opposition to outside influences, the firm word (*besa*-promise) often meant mutual protection.

The symbiosis that engulfed the clans of different ethnicity was noticeable and evident until more recently, and traces of it can be found even today. A French traveler was taken aback, when in the late years of the 18th century he visited Hercegovina. It was the Christian holiday of St. Ilija, but to his amazement he noticed that Moslems were going to the mosque, splendidly lit. His agitated curiosity and inquiry were given a laconic answer: "It's Ilija in the

morning, Alija in the evening!" Even today one can still
see Albanian Moslems of Kosovo, Metohija, or Macedonia,
men, women, and children of the same family, descending
from their hills and visiting a Serbian monastery. Men wear-
ing their white skullcaps, in their white serge trousers
braided with black lace, followed by their women (who no
longer wear veils), bringing their infant children or alone,
waiting for the priest to admit them to the Serbian place
of worship. They arrive in reverence of Holy Mother, or a
saint whose icon is in the church or, more often, of relics
of some Serbian king, sanctified in the monastery and
known to help where Mohammed and Esculap had failed.
"No wonder," a Serbian priest would comment after such
visits (always on Friday), "they were Christians once."

In the 14th and 15th centuries, the great majority of
Albanians were Christians, Eastern Orthodox or Roman
Catholic in the North, predominately Eastern Orthodox in
the South. Members of the north Albanian tribe, Malisori,
celebrated Saint Nikola Day (their patron and protector,
just as he is of the Montenegrins). Both could be heard singing their national ballads, to the accompaniment of the one-
string instrument (gusle). The Malisori would sing about
King Marko and Prince Lazar; the Montenegrins would
sing about Skanderbeg, alias George Castriota.

It is an exceptional case today, but until recently it was
not unusual to see Albanians visiting with their Christian
friends on Christian holidays, or participating in dancing
and feasting (wine and pork avoided), attending weddings
and baptism ceremonies. Usually these were the traditional
inter-family ties of friendship, hailing from the old days,
when the respective families were closely knit, living
through periods of harmony or quarrels, but never inimical hostility. These were the days of stable family life,
when young men went abroad only to return with money
saved, and then continued to live the life of their fathers.
Even today there are young Schipetars (Albanians) who
remember that their fathers would never begin any project
on Tuesday, the day of the Kosovo defeat.

The monastery of Pech, which was the seat of the Serbian Patriarch (1346-1556 and 1557-1766), maintained close and friendly relations with the Albanians of the rugged area of Rugovo, which provided shelter to Patriarch Arsenius IV in 1737, when he had to hide from the pursuing Turks. These Albanians continued to provide guard services to the Patriarchate in Pech and the Dechani Monastery, but in recent years with notable lack of success.

Late in the 19th century two English ladies visited Kosovo (Miss Muir Mackenzie and Miss A. P. Irby). In their book, *Travels in the Slavonic Provinces of Turkey-in-Europe,* they reported the respect among Albanians for the Serbian holy places. The authors blamed the Turks and their propaganda for any Albanian excesses that occasionally took place in the area. They maintained that the Turks were the ones who incited young Moslem Albanians to ill-treat the Serbs, to "throw stones and filth" at Serbian funerals, and to shout "insults and obscenities at Christians on Sundays."

But it was not only the Turks who were the source of such incidents. Other quarters (e.g. Rome and Vienna) contributed their bit to poison the atmosphere in Kosovo, Metohija, and the border area between Montenegro and the Albanian regions. Both Italy and Austro-Hungary had no interest in maintaining peace and harmony in those regions.

While one should never underestimate the importance of foreign schemes in muddling relations between the Slavs and the Moslems in the area, the phenomenon of Islamization, and all that it meant in terms of personal welfare and social advancement, still remained the main cause of the estrangement. To the Albanians, Islam was an opportunity that they could not let pass. It was a vehicle, not only to get even, but in addition to outrank the Greeks and the Slavs.

The Islamization process was a continuous one, but its fervor and intensity were not. At certain periods, in certain areas, with certain people, the process would explode, usually triggered by some violent event. Something would happen, such as Albanians siding with Venice in a dispute with the Porte, or the Serbs would join the Austrian army in its incursions into the territory. The aftermath would be intensified Islamization. Pressures would be applied, and on such occasions Serbs would usually show more intransigence than Albanians. The Albanians could never understand that inherent Serbian hostility toward the Turks, but then they had no Kosovo in their heritage. The Greeks, on the other hand, understood it very well; they had Thermopylae.

One must credit all Balkan peoples with one thing: capacity for survival. But some did it the hard way; others compromised and adapted to what they regarded as a temporary situation. Even today, modern history has proved that Serbs fall into the first category. The Kosovo syndrome seemingly does not let them act in any other way.

Albanians are survivors, too, but in most cases they do it the easier way. Islamization was one such way. The phenomenon of "crypto Christianity," practiced profusely by many Albanians, both Catholic and Orthodox, is proof. This cannot be said, however, to be a character trait of Albanians, or even duplicity, but rather a pragmatic solution of an intelligent survivor. Again we come to the question: could not the Serbs have done the same thing? Yes, and those who were not burdened with Kosovo did it (the Bosnians).

American historian Stavro Skendi defines the Albanian crypto-Christians as follows: "The crypto Christians lived in regions near those inhabited by Moslems and professed Islam, but satisfied their consciences by practicing Christianity in private. They emerged in periods of outbursts of anti-Christian fanaticism" (*The Albanian National Awakening;* Princeton, 1967, p. 12). Skendi continues: "In the North the crypto Christians were concentrated in the

Pashalik of Prizren; they were called *laramanë* (motley) and they lived chiefly around Ipek (Pech) and in the plain of Kosovo." Miss Mackenzie called these Albanians "secret Christians." She cited a case, in those border areas where Albanians and Montenegrins lived, of a young Albanian Moslem letting the Serbian priest into his house, because his parents were still clinging to the old faith, while he himself was a hybrid.

There was another religous phenomenon in Albania, mostly in the southern areas, with the same rationale. The Moslem sect of Bektashism (a product of Anatolia), as early as the 13th century, existed in the frontier regions where Christianity, Islam, and paganism coexisted. Bektashis were not so much anti-Christian as they were pro-Albanian. They proclaimed themselves to be brothers of all peoples, which is why the Slavs preferred the Bektashis to the Sunni converts. The latter, however, were more numerous than the Bektashis in the regions of Kosovo, Montenegro, Hercegovina, and Bosnia.

The Sunni fervor prompted the puritanical Montenegrin Prince-Bishop Danilo (1670-1735) to purge converted Montenegrins. In their Moslem fanaticism, the latter had gone so far as to assist the invading Turkish force to enter the Montenegrin capital of Cetinje. National bards sing of the brothers Martinovich who executed the eerie plan of eradicating the traitorous "poturice" (converts) with their consecrated maces. It was done in the dark of one Christmas eve (1702). This crepuscular feat immensely impressed Russian Tsar Peter the Great. He ordered money, gifts, missals, and icons to be sent to the Prince Bishop of Montenegro.

The massacre resulted from an intense hatred of everything Moslem, including people of their own blood who had converted to Islam. As a young man of 20, when he attained power, Danilo Petrovich-Njegosh, felt rather strongly that one day the Moslem corruption of Montenegrin Christian souls would have to be stopped. That day came when the Pasha of Skadar promised him safe conduct to Podgoritsa, where he was to consecrate a new church. Danilo did not trust Turkish promises, but felt that "for the sake of my faith, I have to go, though it may be my fate not to return." He saddled his best horse and departed. On his way back, Bishop Danilo was blackmailed. The Pasha demanded 3,000 ducats for his release to the Montenegrins. As he was being marched back to Cetinje, he must have thought of a suitable revenge. The ransom was somehow paid, and Danilo summoned his flock to agree on the day when the traitorous Turks would be massacred all over the country. The executioners were merciless; all those who refused baptism were executed, and Montenegrins have ever since sung about this feat of "purification." Traitors were no more in their ranks. And the neighboring Albanians, if of Moslem faith, never lost sight of the bloody message.

Bishop Danilo's type of solution, regardless of how drastic and effective in Montenegro, could not stop the process of Islamization in the Balkans. The only viable opposition was in the fortitude of the Christian people themselves, in their resolution to oppose Islam and to "die for the Christian faith" if necessary. Albanians obviously felt that choosing death would be impractical. Once they found that conversion to Islam was a valuable asset, they could not be stopped. By the end of the 17th century, two-thirds of them were Moslems. The Turks were at the peak of their might, and their corruptive policy of granting favors and privileges to individuals and tribes that accepted Islam prevented all attempts to solidify any meaningful mass resistance.

In a sense, Albanians found the special treatment they got from the Turks, once they converted to Islam, not unusual. They were treated as a separate category in Byzantine and in Serbian times. Their warriors were in great demand, and one of the ablest generals that Tsar Dushan had at the time of his Greek campaign was an Albanian by origin.

Dushan settled many Albanians in conquered lands as a reward for their services. Not only as mercenaries, but as a sheep and other livestock raising ethnic group, the Albanians enjoyed a special and separate status.

By the 19th century, in areas where Serbs and Albanians were inter-relating, something more critical than ethnic or religious differences was becoming evident as an impediment to communication between them. This was the disparity in political outlooks or concepts. The Serbs had a very clear idea about Serbian statehood, while the Albanians, with occasionally weak blimps of Albanianism, were for the most part Turkish oriented. While the Serbs dreamed of their Serbian state, the Albanians tended to identify with the Ottoman Empire of which they were a part.

Albanian patriot Sami bey Frasheri, in his history of Albania, written in Turkish in 1899 and later translated into German, describes the Albano-Turkish affinity in the following words: "Turks were finding devout and courageous co-fighters in Albanians, while Albanians found the Turkish kind of governing very much to their taste. In Turkish times, Albania was a wealthy and blossoming country, because Albanians were riding together with Turks in war campaigns all over the world, and were returning with rich booty, gold and silver, costly arms, and fine horses from Arabia, Kurdistan, and Hungary." (*Was war Albanien, was ist es, was wird es werden* [What was Albania, what is it, what will it be]: Vienna and Leipzig, 1913, p. 12).

Warring and fighting, the Islamic converts developed an aggressive mentality, and in times of peace turned on their Christian neighbors. They began viewing themselves as the propagators of the Islamic faith. Much better armed than the deprived Christians, they left a bloody trail in their forceful Islamization drives among the Serbs. An old Serbian religious inscription, made in 1574, reads: "This is where great Albanian violence took place, especially by Mehmud Begovich in Pech, Ivan Begovich in Skadar,

Sinnan-Pashich Rotulovich in Prizren, Slad Pashich in Djako-vitsa—they massacred two thousand Christians. . . . Have Mercy upon us, Oh Lord, Look down from Heaven and free your flock" (translated from Ljubomir Stojanović, *Stari Srpski zapisi i natpisi* [Old Serbian Inscriptions and Epitaphs] : Vol. I, p. 219, Belgrade, 1902). There in the same vein are numerous other memorials or inscriptions in Stojanovich's collection.

Probably the most notorious among the converts was Koukli beg and his offspring who used force in their at-tempts to Islamize the area of Pastrik, Has, and Opolje at the end of the 18th century. Remembered as an arch enemy of the Serbs is another Islamic convert, Grand Vizier Sinan Pasha, who ordered the remains of Saint Sava trans-ferred from the Milesheva Monastery to Belgrade and there burned on a wooden pyre in 1594. In his rage he reasoned that once turned into ashes, Sava's body would cease being a rallying point for Serbian Christendom. Blinded by his new faith, he never realized that his enemies were not guided by Sava's flesh but by his spirit and his ideals.

Ever since the Christians began fighting for their faith in Roman times, they were the deprived ones. And in Turkish times the deprived status would have been acceptable philosophically to the Christians, had the Albanians also been among the deprived segments of the population, even if they showed signs of enmity toward the Serbs. But to abandon the faith of ones ancestors, in order to join the privileged class, was not acceptable. This is why the quality of animosity between Serbs and Bulgars was always con-siderably different from the quality of estrangement be-tween Serbs and Albanians. This is not to judge or to moralize, but simply to emphasize the qualitative differ-ence in the two hostilities.

# CHAPTER V

## MIGRATIONS, ETHNIC VACUUM,
## SHIFTS IN CENTER OF SERBDOM

No history of Serbo-Albanian relations can be complete without special attention to the events that took place in the second half of the 17th and the first half of the 18th centuries. It was a period of migrations, of continuous mobility, voluntary or forced, manifested in either individual or group decisions to leave home and settle somewhere else. These processes tended to be intensified and to become more evident in times of social upheavals or wars, but they were part of life.

Around the beginning of the 17th century, German commanders of the Austrian border areas (today's Slavonia and Croatia) were luring Christian peasants from Serbia and Bosnia to settle in the vacant but fertile areas, and to "fight for the Cross." This whole region was considered a military district, under the administration of the Vienna government, and was exempt from any other authority. New settlers were promised a high degree of autonomy, religious freedom, and free election of their own local chiefs (knezes). Local feudal masters, including the Croatian families of Zrinski and Frankopan, were not happy with this arrangement. They wanted their lands protected and defended, but not at the price of losing their feudal benefits. The new settlers—mostly Serbs—resisted the landlords' demands, claiming that the Emperor had "invited" them and "promised" them special status. The commanders sided with the settlers. Whatever tactic the Austrian Emperor used—setting up commissions, mediators, special status arrangements—to resolve the issue, Serbian settlers, at least in the early period, usually ended up victorious.

The ugly reality developing in front of all concerned, however, consisted of local nobles, the Papacy, and the Imperial Austrian Court fighting for the bodies and souls of the new arrivals. Details of that long and sinister fight are not the subject of this study, but suffice it to say that the seeds sown by the main participants in that game would poison the Serbo-Croatian atmosphere for many decades to come.

The Ottoman rulers, for their part, did not abandon their expansionist plans, in spite of occasional setbacks in military campaigns. In the midst of persistent "try again tactics" it was becoming painfully obvious that the Turkish "bites" were getting bigger and bigger. And the whole concept of the "militarized zone" along the rivers that separated Europe from the Balkans, grew in importance. But the idea of attracting new soldiers by offering them land was not an Austrian monopoly. The Turks did the same thing, using the same idea. The only difference was the ethnicity of prospective settlers; they chose Albanians. Consequently, for every Christian that the Austrians got out of the Balkan area, the Turks brought in an Albanian Moslem.

In a sense, by inviting Christian Serbs to cross the river, Austria was de-Christianizing the Balkans. There is enough evidence to show that the Turks were not particularly interested in clearing the area of the Serbian element, because the Turkish authorities had tried in advance to counter the ensuing panic among the terrified Slavs, by promising fair treatment, pardons, amnesty, and retention of their old status. But the Slavs could not trust the Turks, especially not the Janissaries. Moreover, the Serbs had usually involved themselves with Christian armies' incursions so deeply that it would have been naive to take the Turkish promises seriously.

To the Turkish brothers-in-arms, the Albanians, those northbound Slav migrations were a real blessing. They would not wait twice for the invitation to fill the vacuum. Consequently, the Islamization of the Slav territories went steadily onward. The Albanian tribes of Malisoris and Dukadjins were descending from their mountains, encouraged by the Turks to push east and north along the valleys and main roads. Serbian ethnographers and social science experts and politicians have presented detailed studies of the "main migratory routes" (Jovan Cvijich, Stojan Novakovich, Jovan Tomich, Stanoje Stanojevich, Jovan Hadzi, Vasiljevich—to mention a few). Malisoris were mainly entering the Kosovo-Metohija area, but they also went to the areas of Novi Pazar and Sjenitsa. The Dukadjins went eastward and spilled over into the Vardar-Morava corridor, reaching as far as Leskovats.

It is rather positively established that the first Albanians to come to the Kosovo area were either still of the Christian religion—in most cases Roman Catholic—or recently converted, with their wives still of the Christian faith. The first "waves" were not hard core Moslem elements. Apparently these were individuals who either found it increasingly difficult to save their Christian faith in the Turkish environment, and wanted to move into areas of religiously "mixed" population, or they were recent converts who did not yet feel comfortable with Islam.

Roman Catholic bishops, seated in coastal cities but whose ecclesiastical jurisdiction extended inland, have left ample evidence of this migratory process, and reported on ethnic and religious changes occurring in the region. Archbishops, priests, and friars visited cities such as Prizren,

Prishtina, Skoplje, Djakovitsa, invariably commenting on the increased Albanian presence. Marion Bizzi (1610), Giorgie Bianchi (1614), the two Masareks (of Albanian descent—Peter in 1623 and Matej in 1764 and 1767), Matej Benlich (1615), Josip Berisha (1782), and many others travelled up and down the region and left behind perspicuous notes and travelogues of great value, which make for fascinating reading. Bianchi found Prizren to be "the prettiest city of Serbia," while Benlich calls Prizren "capo di Servia." Most of them mention Serbian monasteries, especially "chiesa bellisima" of Dechani and Grachanitsa, as well as "sedia patriarcale" of Pech, "dove si trove un corpo santo del re Milutin de Servia" (Marion Bolica, 1614). Archbishop Matej Masarek (1760) saw numerous graves and burial sites of slain Serbs ("sepolture de scismatici et altri da essi uccisi"). Moslem Albanians excelled in viciousness, reports the Archbishop, because they feel that being Moslem gives them the right to do anything they want ("perche sono Turchi e possono farsi ogni male che li piace"). He also noticed (in 1774) that cities were full of "Macedoni" and "Albanesi Turchi." Villages have only a few Christians, he reported, because most had fled to Germany, Wallachia, Sofia or elsewhere.

Similar in tone and factual content are a few reports that are known to have been sent to Russia, or submitted to Russian emissaries, by Orthodox clergy. For example, Patriarch Vasilije Brkich wrote to the commander of the visiting Russian Naval Expedition in Kotor, Admiral Alexis Orlov (1771): "Albanians arrived, became Turks and filled all towns and villages, took the land and enriched themselves enormously."

The Austro-Turkish and Russo-Turkish wars in the 17th and 18th centuries had traumatic consequences for the Serbian population in the Balkans, because in every case expeditions proved to be a false alarm. Every raising of new hopes was followed by subsequent disappointment, suffering and despair. It takes an enormous, unfathomable

reservoir of national resilience to surmount shocks and de-
pressions that followed every disappointment. In those,
probably the most difficult times in Serbian national history, the best of the Serbian Church rose to the surface,
and carried out its inspirational role to a remarkable degree.

A nation brutally beaten, a nation enslaved, a nation beheaded of leadership, and robbed of literacy, turned to its
primitive monks and national bards. As if unimpressed by
the enormity of the task, they suddenly found themselves
being a depository and source of national hope. The monasteries as religious centers suddenly became national
centers. This very Church, which once insisted on having
two separate and powerful centers, spiritual and secular,
in one nation, now had to take both jobs.

Ill-equipped, inexperienced, and scared to death, the
patriarchs seated at the Pech Monastery of Saint Savior
(Svetoga Spasa) indeed saved their nation. In the period
1557-1766, they stood their ground until chased away,
but as they were forced to migrate they carried their mission with them. Dr. Djoko Slijepchevich, historian and
prominent connoisseur of Serbian Orthodoxy, quotes a
number of authoritative names of men who dealt with this
subject: linguist Vuk Stefan Karadzich, historian Vladimir
Chorovich, ethnographer Jovan Cvijich, historian Stanoje
Stanojevich—all of them analyzed this intricate trans-
formation that had taken place in the thinking processes
of Church leaders who assumed the responsibility of
shouldering secular leadership.

Slijepchevich has so well characterized them (in quotes
or paraphrases of the above-mentioned authors): They still
wore their ecclesiastical robes; they always wore the signs
of priestly dignity—censers, crosses, and shepherd's rods,
but the Serbian people did not bow to them as sextons,
but as rulers. In enslaved Serbia, the priest was not a clergy-
man, but judge, administrator, counsellor, guardian of the
national idea, historian, teacher—everything that the priest
did not do in the Serbian state. And when the Serbs kissed

his hand, they did not do it out of reverence or faith, but out of respect which is shown to a national leader. The patriarch ceased being a shepherd and became leader of highwaymen, rebels. He continued to wear the cross, but the Serbs looked to the hand that held the national seal. He spoke of the Heavenly Tsar, but the Serbs asked about earthly tsars. The Orthodox religion, continues Slijepche-vich, lost its churchly dogmatic character, and increasingly accepted an *ethnic* character and thus became the *Serbian* church. It was an integral part of the national spirit just as folklore is an integral part of that spirit, concludes Slijep-chevich (*Srpsko-arbanaški odnosi kroz vekove sa posebnim osvrtom na novije vreme* [Serbo-Albanian Relations Through the Centuries, with Special Reference to More Recent Times]; Himmelsthur, West Germany, 2nd ed., 1983), pp. 139-140.

The Montenegrins did not have to go through this period of adjustment, because their metropolitan at Cetinje was the leader of the nation as Prince-Bishop. When their see became hereditary (1697) in the Petrovich family, the sense of unity of the nation enhanced the morale of the country as a whole, and among the Great Powers it raised the image of its relevance.

The one thing that helped the Serbs adjust to the new situation was the fact that the idea of an autocephalous Patriarchate was well established in the conscience of the Serbs before the state organization was eradicated. Before it collapsed, the Serbian state had two separate centers of influence. And while that might have seemed divisive at that time, it turned out to be a cohesive factor when one of these centers was removed. Serbs had only to narrow the focus. Ever since Byzantine times, the Patriarch was a highly respected and visible authority. Tsar Dushan made it that way, copying Byzantine custom. The Patriarch al-ways wore his insignias of power, always signed documents in green ink, traveled with his entourage on horseback, and was given all formal respect due to a national leader. We know that Tsar Dushan, when John Cantacusenus visited him in Prishtina, met his eminent guest by dismounting and holding his horse. This is how Dushan would meet his Patriarch, too, the one that he practically appointed. Undoubtedly, such respect, given by the Tsar of such national repute and esteem, helped national attention to center on the spiritual leader when there were no more Dushans around.

The Serbian name and presence became a household word, as the Islamic-Christian bout (Austro-Turkish wars) was raging in the 17th and 18th centuries. The very fact that the Serbs were in the frontier areas became a factor in the military and political planning of the contending armies. Although supposedly leaderless, the Serbs had to be viewed as either potential allies or enemies. In vying for the attention of the Patriarch, the Christian forces had the advantage by virtue of a common faith. But the Turks needed the Patriarch as a factor of stability among the Serbian Christian masses in the territory under Islamic rule. Subsequently, when the Patriarchate was removed from the scene (1766), the Turks turned more to the Greeks for that stability.

As the series of Austro-Turkish wars developed, the fluid situation became too tempting for the impatient Serbs to stand by. The Turks would push north and west into the Panonian plain, then retreat south, either because of defeats or a need to rush home to quell Janissary rebellions, with the Austrians in hot pursuit. Every time this happened, the temptation for the Serbs to join the Austrians and the Slavs fighting in their ranks became irresistable. Then when the tables would be turned, with the Austrians retreating, the Serbs would face a dilemma: wait for the revengeful Islamites or start marching north, leaving everything behind.

In 1663-64, Mehmed Chuprilich, an able Turkish military strategist of Albanian descent, pushed north to within 100 miles of Vienna, but was defeated at St. Gothardt.

Twenty years later, when the famous Turkish Grand Vizier
Kara Mustafa, reached all the way to Vienna and kept it
under seige for months, the fate of the whole of Europe
was at stake, and not only that of the Balkan Christians.
To the Serbs, the siege had a special meaning, because it
took place near the third centennial of the battle of Kosovo.

While all of this was happening, there was no unity
among the "defenders of Christianity," the Western European Great Powers. Even when Kara Mustafa was tighten-
ing the noose and strangling the Austrian capital, France
and Spain were not coming to the aid of the besieged. To
the Slavs of the Balkans the picture was familiar. And to
the invading Turks it must have seemed an inherent character trait of Christians. From the time that Orchan
brought them to Europe, the Turks never saw Christians
unite when faced by danger.

Then, of all people, a Slav King, John (Jan) Sobieski of
Poland (resented by germanic central Europe), changed his
foreign policy views, and came to the aid of besieged
Prince Starhemberg. Sobieski delivered an irreparable blow
to the strange coalition of Turks and Hungarians, a blow
that enabled Eugene of Savoy to begin his big chase. He
beat the Turks at Petrovaradin (1716), and a year later at
Belgrade, where Grand Vizier Mustafa Pasha met his death.
It is said that Mustafa Pasha was an alcoholic and an in-
competent general, which makes one wonder what would
have been the fate of Europe if, instead of Mustafa Pasha,
the Sultan had an Evrenos-bey as did Murad at Kosovo.
And one tends to be horrified when he tries to vizualize
what would have happened to Western Civilization had not
John Sobieski·reversed his thinking.

Some time after the siege of Vienna, the Turks defeated
the Austrians at Katchanik, and once more the Serbs were
joining the latter in a northward retreat. The Austrian army,
under General Piccolomini, had not endeared itself to the
Serbs. While in Skoplje, the general burned Tsar Dushan's
one-time capital, allegedly in a move to save himself and

his soldiers from the plague. But his death and the decision to retreat left the Serbs no choice. Once again, 300 years after the battle of Kosovo, the Serbs were withdrawing from that familiar plain. This time, however, they did not leave their leader dead on the field. Patriarch Arsenius III decided to retreat at the head of his flock (1690). The scene was later immortalized in a huge painting by the Serbian painter, Paja Jovanovich (1896). Arsenius left Pech and led some 35,000 Serbian families toward their new home. Many joined the exodus enroute, and after a brief assembly and parleys with the Austrians in Belgrade, they finally settled in what was later to be called Vojvodina. The Serbs were hoping and naively dreaming of founding an autonomous "free" Serbian state, but the Austrians had no intention of letting them do it.

It should be noted that the next Austrian advance in 1714 gave the population of upper Serbia (Shumadija) a respite from Turkish rule for more than two decades. The Habsburgs even added the name of "Serbia" to their crown title, and the Serbian militia assisted in maintaining peace and order in the region. After Austrian military misfortunes and the Peace of Belgrade (1739), however, the Serbs were once again on the move. The Serbs, who had gone south as far as Novi Pazar, once again had to leave the heartland of Old Serbia, this time under the leadership of Arsenius IV. Another 30,000 or so Serbian families moved out. Hence, two massive migrations in less than half a century left a lot of Serbian land as vacant territory.

Moreover, this time the return of the Turks seemed even more painful. One of the reasons was that in this period of fifty years the awareness of Turkish internal weaknesses had grown, with the consequent decline in the power of the central government and its ineffectiveness in controlling local power structures. Under the circumstances, numerous "sipahis" (Moslems who held military fiefs), and the land-possessing beys (who ran "chiftlicks") began acting as local  tyrants. The plight of those who cultivated the land (Christians, in this case Serbs) was compounded by the fact that they had no one to represent them. The Patriarch had left, and soon the Patriarchate itself was officially abolished in 1766.

The Porte was not in a hurry to abolish the Patriarchate itself, but the Greek Patriarch in Constantinople felt that the Serbian Orthodox flock should not be left without some support in the face of intensified Islamization. At first he "volunteered" several bishops, and then he offered an attractive price for the right of representation. The Porte accepted, and the Greek Orthodoxy took over both the Pech and Ohrid dioceses. The Serbs were not comfortable with the new religious protectorate, for two reasons: they were not used to foreigners in religious matters, and they were sure that indirectly the Greeks would recoup the money they had paid to the Porte for the right to represent the Serbs. But, in the long run, it was a fortunate development, because the spiritual vacuum that was created by the abolition of the Serbian Patriarchate was filled by the lesser of two evils.

Hellenic-oriented priests were resented by both Serbian and Albanian Orthodox believers, but where else could they find people of knowledge and adequate culture to enlighten them in this darkness? Where else could Orthodox Russia find a tangible organization to be used in the large program of "protecting the Sultan's Christian subjects?" The last thing that the Greeks wanted was a Slav "protector;" but how does one turn him down? By turning to the Mohammedan Sultan?

As the Orthodox population of Serbian and Albanian regions came under the jurisdiction of the Patriarchate of Constantinople, it meant—based on the Turkish concept of "millet"—that not only church matters, but education of the Christians as well, would become the responsibility of the Greeks. Yet, who but the Greeks, among Balkan Christians of that time, were qualified for the job of such

importance? Whatever literacy there was left among the
Christians of the Balkans was in the hands (and heads) of
the Greek Orthodoxy.

As for the relationship between Serbs and Albanians,
the abolishing of the Serbian Patriarchate had devastating
consequences. Conversion to Islam was increased and ever
more pushed upon the Serbian population. Djoko Slijepchevich is right when he writes that with regard to en-
larging the Moslem community in the Serbian regions, it
was not important whether they were new Serbian or new
Albanian Moslem converts. Both of them accepted the
Turkish statehood idea. And with no Pech Patriarchate to
propagate the Serbian statehood idea (obviously the Greek
clergy would not do it), the Serbian national concept was
in mortal danger. Slijepchevich calls this period "the second
Kosovo," which in comparison with the first was twice as
bad. For the Serbs, in addition to political subjugation,
they were now faced with spiritual estrangement as well.
The "phanariot" ideology of Greek priests and teachers
could hardly be considered as tailored to fit the Slav concept of nationhood.

Fortunately, at this difficult and trying time for the
Serbs, the second center of Serbianism, Montenegro, was
able to pick up the fallen Serbian standard. Regardless of
how tiny and insignificant as a lighthouse, Montenegro was
the last remaining Serbian beacon, and it was important
for several reasons. First, it meant that the light had not
been extinguished. Second, it had a powerful Slav provider
in Moscow. Third, it was not in Sremski Karlovtsi (on Austrian territory). Fourth, it was in the immediate vicinity of
Albanian and Turkish Islamism. Last, but not least, Montenegrin leaders had not for a moment abandoned the ideal
of Serbian resurrection. They had always considered themselves as the only legitimate heirs of Serbian statehood.
After all, was it not Nemanja, the son of their own
land (Zeta), who in the 12th century founded the Serbian
state in Rascia and its famous dynasty? "The most Serbian
of all Serbian lands" is what Montenegro called itself.

Montenegrins are fanatically patriotic. Their state was in fact a theocracy in its purest form. When the last member of the Crnojevich dynasty left the Black Mountain early in the 16th century and went to Venice to live, he transferred his whole country to the Bishop of Cetinje. This is when the inseparability of the altar and the throne became the law of the land. The Prince Bishop was elected from among the monks at Cetinje, and was consecrated by the Serbian Patriarch in Pech (later Sremski Karlovtsi). The Petrovich family ruled that way until the middle of the 19th century. As long as the church and government were in one body, Christianity was fiercely pitted against Islam. An administrator could bring himself to negotiate with the Moslems, but a priest could never be expected to take such a sacrilegious step. He was an eternal enemy of Islam, and anything else would constitute a betrayal of the Christian faith.

A loosely bound coalition of tribes and clans, similar to the Albanian pattern, Montenegrins had a much more developed sense of belonging to one nation than the Albanians had. In times of danger, this sense of mission and the hatred of Turks would outrank all personal and tribal feuds. A Russian observer (would he be called a military adviser today?) said of Montenegrins that it is "just impossible to keep them in reserve," and that they cannot calmly "bear the view of a Moslem." Montenegrins were specialists in guerrilla warfare—ambushes, scouting, and surprise attacks—and would leap at the enemy like "wolves on a white flock." All this at a time when their Serbian brothers were abandoning the homeland and moving north, or helplessly watching the cover of impregnable darkness falling upon their name and heritage.

The Serbian bastion was in a fight to the death against Moslems, and during the 18th century any Turk approaching the boundaries of Montenegro knew for certain that he would be fired upon without warning. This enmity could not but negatively affect relations with Albanians as well.

Russian support, the fact that Russia explicitly recognized the independence of Montenegro a century and a
half before the Great Western Powers did, represented an
enormous boost to the morale of the "warriors of the
Black Mountain." The Montenegrin ballad expresses it
well when it relates how Montenegrins reacted to the letter of Peter the Great, calling upon them to fight against
the Crescent. At the words of the "Slav Tsar," Montenegrins "all brandish their sabres and run to their muskets."
When they had to face the enemy in battle, the Bishop
would "bless them and sprinkle them with holy water."
The Bishop himself would lead his warriors to victory
(Bishop Danilo was wounded in the battle against the Turk
in 1712). The ballad says: "Oh brother Serbs, and all of
you who have free hearts in your breasts, rejoice, for the
ancient liberty will not perish so long as we hold the Black
Mountain." In 1715, Bishop Danilo went to Petersburg
and came back with encouraging promises, subsidies, and
material aid in general. Montenegrins won another victory
against the Turks in 1727, with the Bishop—Montenegrins
say—disposing of twenty-two Turks "with his own sword."
Slav cooperation between small Montenegro and its mighty
protector enhanced the prestige of Orthodoxy in that area,
as well as abroad, so much so that the local Venetian
prelate of Antivari (Bar) sent home a number of reports
expressing worry about the proselytising influence of the
Montenegrin bishopric.

Throughout the century which for the Serbs represented
a second Kosovo, Montenegrin bishops were defying the
Turkish usurper. In 1754 they battled against the Bosnian
vizier who demanded tribute and "the twelve most beautiful girls on Black Mountain." The Montenegrin Bishop
(Sava) replied defiantly. According to the national ballad,
his reply read: "The tribute we will send thee will be a
stone from our soil, and instead of the twelve virgins, thou
shalt receive twelve pig's tails with which thou mayest
adorn your turban!" In 1768, Montenegrins managed to

repulse, at great human loss, three separate Turkish task forces invading the country. The following year, Austrian Empress Maria Theresa gave assurance of support to the mountaineers.

In 1796, Turkish troops were routed in the narrow pass of Kruze. And during the Napoleonic wars, between 1805 and 1810, Montenegrins did whatever they could to support Russia's efforts in stalling the French advance. And in 1820, Bishop Peter I, managed to inflict another defeat upon the Turks, chasing them out of the valley of the Zeta.

When their neighbor, Mahmud Pasha Bushatlija of Skadar, started a rebellion against the central Ottoman governmen while at the same time displaying open pretensions to Serbian territories (late in the 18th century he had sent his private army to Kosovo and entered Prishtina), this Northern Albanian touched the most sensitive Montenegrin nerve. The metropolitan, Petar Petrovich-Njegosh I (1782-1830) knew he would have to face this enemy squarely. And a paramount enemy he was. Mahmud Pasha had wealth, power, ambition (even royal ambitions eventually), and through a combination of threat, bribe, and persuasion he was able to become practically the overlord of northern Albania. French officers were training his army, Austrian agents were financing his military build-up.

In spite of all his power, Mahmud Pasha was not able to establish his claim that he represented the Albanian people. His army was a motley crew of mercenaries, sincere Albanian nationalists, and blackmailed Montenegrin tribes. In spite of temporary victories and successful local military campaigns against Montenegrins, in the two final battles in July and September 1796, he ran into a solid wall of opposition by a united and inspired small nation, which had a clear perception of its mission.

Montenegrins fought for an idea: Albanians for a rebellious man. Montenegrins had a broad national concept: the Albanians a narrow provincial interest. Mahmud Pasha was captured in the second battle, his head cut off and taken to the metropolitan. It can still be seen in Cetinje. The one important consequence of this Montenegrin victory was the respect and attention that this small nation gained in Constantinople. It meant, also, the consolidation of internal authority of the metropolitan. And it enhanced the symbolic image of Montenegro as a defender of the Christian faith in the Balkans. Metropolitan Peter I utilized Montenegro's position to communicate with Serbian intellectuals abroad, notably in Vojvodina (with Dositej Obradovich, David Nerandzich, Sava Tekelija), all of whom agreed that there was need to form one all-Slav state in the Balkans.

Being the Albanians' closest neighbors, Montenegrins believed that they understood them better than anyone else. The two societies were aware of similarities—both having traditional values and patriarchal views. They were of different races and in the case of most of them of different religious faiths. But these factors were not the basic apple of discord between them. The main difference was in their different perceptions of Constantinople. To the Albanians it was the capital of their state; to the Montenegrins it was the center of Serbian oppression. Most damaging in terms of relations between them, however, was the Albanian support to the Turkish forces that fought the Montenegrins. Albanians viewed Montenegro as a Turkish land and its people Turkish subjects. Nothing could have been farther from Montenegrin feelings, who considered their land as "the only territory of Old Serbia still free," and who could be subjects only of Montenegro or Serbia. That is why, even in moments when Albanian leaders would later on find sanctuary at Cetinje, the minds of the host and the visitors could never meet.

# CHAPTER VI

## THE SERBIAN REVOLUTION AND ALBANIANS

At the beginning of the 19th century the Balkan peninsula was a "powder keg" and Serbia with its uprisings
(1804 and 1815) was the "fuse." The Serbs were soaring
upward, carried on the wings of national liberation, and
the Greeks were not far behind. The Albanians, pulled
down by the weight of the aging Ottoman Empire, nevertheless realized that the Serbs and Greeks could not be
held down. Should they try to stop the Serbs or should
they join them and turn against Constantinople? They
were undecided, mainly for reasons discussed in the previous chapter.

To the Serbs, the uprising under their peasant leader,
"Black George" (Karadjordje), was a repeat performance
of what the Serbs did under Nemanja some seven long
centuries earlier. They realized that with the "sick man" in
Constantinople, the moment for the leap to independence
was at hand. But to the Albanians any "leap" would have
had to be out of Constantinople, where they were providing honor guards for the Sultan, and performing many
administrative tasks. The Serbs were in their days of
Genesis; the Albanians felt carried by the flood of a

73

terminal Deluge. Would the two nations, which earlier had had a hard time finding a common language, be able to join hands now? The Great Powers, for different reasons, were not interested in having Albanians and Serbs living in peace. Austria wanted to build an Albanian wall between the Serbs and Montenegrins that would prevent their unification. Italy did not want more Slavs in the region of "mare nostrum." Turks wanted to have a Moslem foothold against Austria's southern expansion. Russia was interested in exploiting the Balkan situation so that it could open a second front—if necessary—in its wars against Turkey. The Vatican wanted to complete its long term task of pushing Orthodoxy out of the littoral. For the Balkan "pawns" it was difficult, if not impossible, to bridge the abyss and resist being sucked into the whirlpool.

In the early part of the 19th century, both Montenegrins and Northern Albanians had their sights fixed on what was happening to the north. For nine crucial years the Serbs battled the Turkish armies (1804-1813), and only two years later after being "pacified" they rose again. These two open insurrections sent shock waves throughout the Balkans and central Europe. Leopold Ranke, a German historian, published a book about these uprisings under the title, *Die Serbische Revolution* (1829). "The Serbian Homer," as he liked to call himself, wrote about the "seeds" that were sown, which raised many eyebrows from Petersburg to London. In those capitals, the "Eastern Question" was now compounded by the "Serbian Question," an unknown factor in international politics.

Overnight, the Serbs got a taste of international politics. The Russians sent a message to their Slav brothers: Just think what you and we can achieve together. To the delight of Karadjordje, a Russian general arrived at the Serbian front with a token force of 1,000 troops. The battle of Shtubik (1807) was their first common military victory against the Turks. But after Austerlitz, as Napoleon tied the hands of the Russians (Peace of Tilsit), the Serbs were left alone to face the unrushing Moslems. Black George was fuming angry at the Russians, and their representative in Belgrade, Rodofinikin, found it advisable to remove himself temporarily from the city by crossing the river to the Austrian town of Zemun. In 1810, Karadjordje sent his delegate, Rado Vuchinich, to Napoleon, who gave him a cold shoulder. In 1813, Karadjordje crossed the river himself as Serbia's dream was crushed.

Nevertheless, in the popular mind, Karadjordje came to be viewed as the avenger of the Serbs' defeat at Kosovo. As the courageous leader of the Serbs' first uprising that was to lead to Serbia's resurrection, he became and remained a Serbian hero, a Serbian George Washington.

It was not any easier for the leader of the second uprising (1815), Milosh Obrenovich. He gathered his peasant "elite" in Takovo and told them it would be tough going. He insisted on one thing: absolute obedience and a final say in decision making. Since he was the one who got them into the mess, and who disposed of substantial means, and was the only one who knew the potential of his secret dealings with the Turks, the "elite" had no choice but to agree. Soon he had domestic challenges to his absolutism, and foreign powers gave him a taste of international politics. When he went to pay his respects to the Sultan—some years after the success of the uprising—whom does he meet at the Bosporus but the Russian ambassador, Buteniev. The Sultan gave Milosh an expensive sabre, a beautiful horse, and six artillery guns; the Russian ambassador invited Milosh "to have lunch on his frigate." The Austrian envoy, not to be outdone, went a step further: he offered as a token of high recognition, to send "one person with appropriate staff to open an office in Belgrade." Flattered, Milosh accepted the offer and informed the Sultan, who agreed, and told Buteniev about it, who "said nothing, but just kept his silence."

Soon the Austrian consul, Mr. Meanevich, arrived in Belgrade, and brought to Milosh not one but two Iron Crosses of the First Order. In no time, the British envoy, "with his personal flag," announced himself. Puzzled, Milosh admits, "I had no idea foreign courts will start sending those consuls." Soon the web of international intrigues was all over the semi-autonomous Turkish province of Serbia. "Never did I want to get rid of the Russians, so that I could join the British," protests the indignant Milosh, "nor is it true that the British ever offered me a million ducats to come over to their side." But Milosh suspected that British Consul Hodges was the source of the rumor, because he was "a person of no character and a blabbermouth."

"My greatest mistake," says Milosh in his memoirs, "was in allowing the representative of Mr. Metternich to come here to open his office . . . but, in spite of all the headaches I had with the consuls, I managed continuously to improve the welfare of my province. . . . "

Milosh apparently did not feel that all foreigners were a "headache," as he cultivated relations with Marashli Ali Pasha, the Vizier of Belgrade who was delegated by the Sultan to formulate the details of Serbia's new status in the Ottoman Empire. In dealing with the Sultan's delegate, Milosh's most powerful "argument" was a discreet but generous bribing. He looked out for the influential, sometimes anti-government Moslems, mainly those who were willing to compromise their allegiance. In this way, Milosh opened one door after another, and obtained what he wanted without spilling the blood of his people.

One Albanian who sought Milosh's friendship was the vizier of Skadar, Mustafa Pasha Bushatlija. He maintained that he was a descendant of the old Montenegrin Crnojevich family, and had dynastic ambitions. He was one of two mighty Albanian pashas (the other being Ali Pasha of Tepelena) who resisted the central Turkish government of Sultan Mahmud II. Both of them were eyeing Milosh's successful tactics, especially since they wanted what Milosh had: a hereditary principality. Montenegro's ruler, Bishop Petar Petrovich-Njegosh I was not enthusiastic about Milosh's dealings with Bushatlija, for obvious reasons: the latter's claim to being a Crnojevich descendant would give him some claim to Montenegrin lands as well.

Milosh clearly grasped the benefits for the Serbian state in any kind of Moslem opposition to Turkish rule. Anyone challenging the power of the Porte could be sure to attract his attention, regardless of motives. The more trouble the Porte faced, the more it would be willing to negotiate with Milosh. When through his correspondence with Mustafa, Milosh learned that the Sultan was requiring Mustafa to send 60,000 Albanians to fight the Russians, Milosh advised stalling tactics, and avoiding direct contacts with Russian troops. The Porte knew of Milosh's correspondence with Bushatlija, through the reports of its own spies, and Milosh almost got into trouble as Mustafa was militarily defeated by a Turkish expeditionary force, when the Russo-Turkish war was over (1829). Due to Austria's intervention Mustafa's life was saved and he continued to live in Constantinople.

This experience made Milosh even more cautious when another Moslemized Christian, Bosnian bey Hussein Gradashchevich, decided to challenge the authority of the Sultan. Hussein came to Kosovo to meet the Sultan's troops (July 1831), and defeated the Turkish "pacification" task force. He looked for help from Milosh, but Milosh did not think Hussein had a chance. Milosh was just winning his first battles in diplomacy with the Turks, and did not want to risk losing the concessions he had already obtained from the Porte. The following year, Hussein was defeated in a battle near Sarajevo, and fled to Austria.

Milosh had no use for Albanians (he used the Turkish term Arnauti), and shared the feeling of most Serbs that they were the worst of all the "Turks." One of Milosh's priorities was to get rid of all the converted Moslems, whether formerly Serbs or Albanians, as soon as possible. Two cities, Chuprija and Aleksinats, seem to have been popular with Albanians. Milosh was resolute, and through a combination of pressures and fiscal compensation, he responded to the pleas of ethnic Turks in Chuprija to help them get rid of the Albanians.

The Serbs made a clear distinction between Turks and Albanians. Turks made up a majority of city dwellers, and were landholders or engaged in crafts. The Albanians were a minority and a sort of Moslem proletariat. Both Turks and Serbs referred to Albanians in terms that were usually reserved for the scum of society. They were called "criminals," "brigands," and "murderers," which did not help in restoring social tranquility and inter-ethnic relations.

In Milosh's time, Turks were leaving en masse. Being men of property or professional skills, they were not paupers and had somewhere to go. Not so the Albanians.

As the 19th century progressed, it became ever more evident that the Moslem "aristocracy" in the Balkans was doomed. The more they realized it, the more evident the gap between the landowners (Turks) and the peasants (Christians). As the peasants liberated themselves from working for Turks, they became individual producers, traded with the cities, and even moved to the cities. Many of them received training in various crafts or otherwise entered commerce. The "Turkish" towns of the Balkans began getting an ever greater segment of Slav professionals. The commercial Christian sections began booming, while the Turkish aristocracy wards were decaying as they were losing their material base. Cities like Skoplje, Prilep, Prizren, Ohrid, Bitolj, Solun were attracting dynamic and aggressive Christian, Jewish, Greek, and Armenian elements.

Economically, the tables were turned against the Turks: in an open society they were losing their land; in the cities they were not securing for themselves the lucrative prospects of the new capitalism on the march. They were sitting there, grumbling, smoking their "chibuks" and drinking coffee, watching Christians taking the initiative. To their dismay, the elegant needle-like minarets were being joined by baroque towers, to them an unbearable sight, spoiling the skyline of "their" Moslem cities.

Albanians, a much more aggressive segment of the Balkan Moslem world, could not just sit by and watch the Christians take over. Yet, they faced a two-front "war." On the one side were the Serbs, cocky and confident, and assertive. On the other front was the Turkish "protector," who dispensed not protection but imposed new restrictions and made new demands and obligations. But Albanians were ill-prepared to stand up to the Serbs and to Constantinople at the same time. They had no central authority to coordinate their actions, no unified ideological philosophy, and no clearly defined national program.

With the passage of time, relations between Serbs and Albanians, instead of becoming more conciliatory, were getting worse. As the Serbian state was growing in size and political importance in Balkans affairs, Albanian fears of "Serbian Imperialism" grew apace. Serbia needed its own port on the Adriatic coast, so that it would not have to depend on Austrian good will for its economic development. The natural way to this port was through Montenegro. Realizing this, Austria in its 19th century diplomatic efforts, tried with partial success to create a political and military zone between the two Serbian states. Albanians were to play a large role in this Austrian scheme. Serbian historian Slobodan Jovanovich says that Albanians had to be "the wall" between the Montenegrins and the Serbs.

Three important men in these two Serbian states were painfully aware of the role assigned to Albania. They were the Montenegrin Prince-Bishop Petar Petrovich-Njegosh II, the Serbian Prince Mihailo Obrenovich, and Serbia's political giant, Ilija Garashanin.

Ruling over the barely literate warriors in the mountains—the aerie of the eagles—was the Miltonian poet, romanticist, and classicist, Petar Petrovich-Njegosh II, the spiritual and secular leader of Montenegro. This tall and handsome man was told of politics: "Pray to God and stick with the Russians," the political credo he heard at the deathbed of his predecessor. Njegosh must have wondered. He must have recalled that as a young man he visited Russia and was well received by Catherine II, but not so well by the mighty Prince Potemkin, who threw him out of the country (Serbian historian Stanoje Stanojevich says that Njegosh "swore never again to set foot on Russian soil").

Njegosh had no love for his Moslemized Slav brothers, and approved of the Christmas eve massacre of the converted Montenegrins, mentioned in a previous chapter. He once wrote to the vizier of Skadar, who was of Slav blood: "When you talk to me as a Bosnian, I am your brother, your friend. But when you talk to me as a stranger, as an Asian, as an enemy of our tribe and our name, to me this is adverse." Njegosh knew that the only lasting thing in this cosmos is change. He knew that once large powers such as Austria and Turkey were toppled, there would be room for the development of a South Slav brotherhood. He spent a good deal of time in the Doge's library in Venice, and had "five or six secretaries transcribing for three weeks everything in the archives that had anything to do with South Slavism." At Cetinje (1845), the English visitor, Sir Gardner Wilkinson, had difficulty in fathoming Njegosh, whose hobby was shooting lemons thrown in the air, and who could elaborate on philosophy and transcendental themes while watching the heads of decapitated Turks on the wall in Cetinje. The visitor from London Tower was horrified!

When asked what he would do if his dream was realized in his lifetime, the Bishop said wistfully: "in that case I would go to my patriarchate in Pech, and Serbian Prince Mihailo to Prizren" (the priest to the See of the Serbian spiritual leader, the seculer ruler to the city of Dushan's aura).

Serbia's Prince Mihailo Obrenovich (Milosh's son), educated abroad and of poetic inclination, was just as much of a romantic, a dreamer, and a compulsive visionary as Njegosh. Slobodan Jovanovich says: "Mihailo's plans were not devoid of fantasies, they were too ambitious and sky-reaching. . . . His belief in the heroism of the Serbian people, his confidence in one general Balkan uprising, his persuasion that the Turkish Empire can be destroyed in one blow—all this is pure political romanticism. . . . Never have Serbs been so proud, and never have they believed so strongly in their own historic mission" (*Druga vlada Miloša i Mihaila* [Second reign of. . . ] Belgrade, 1923, p. 263).

Mihailo's rule was short-lived, but inspirational. In a sense, his appearance reminds one of America's JFK era. He ignited the nationalist flame that spread far beyond the borders of that day's Serbia. It was an all-Slav flame, shared by South Slav young intellectuals, and even by a Roman Catholic Bishop in Djakovo (Croatia), Juraj Strosmayer, who founded the Yugoslav Academy in Zagreb in 1867. The Bishop and the Prince carried on an extensive correspondence on the formation of a "Yugoslav State," and the Slav visitors in Belgrade coffee houses were fraternizing with Serbian youths, verbalizing about the "Balkan federation."

How did Albanians fit into this prevailing mood of Montenegro and Serbia? Not very well, if at all. When one consults the political realist of the caliber of Ilija Garashanin, Mihailo's foreign minister, Albanians were a big "nuisance." Garashanin's name indicated that he was a village man (Garashi), but his thinking was as international as Talleyrand's or Metternich's. He knew that ultimately only "united South Slavs" could prevent foreigners (Austria and Russia) from moving into the vacuum created by the collapse of the Ottoman Empire. He knew the importance of having Greeks and Albanians on the side of the Slavs. He had no illusions about Russian politics in the Balkans, but he could see where Russian and Serbian political interests could coincide.

Garashanin knew that Austria thought otherwise. In 1853 he wrote to his friend, Serbian diplomat Marinovich: "Austria will never support the progress of Serbia. . . . It

would be stupid to think any other way." He was positive
of Austria's inimical attitude, for the simple reason that it
had such a large Slav population within its own borders.
Scared of provocation, Austria would watch out for anything that could stir the Slavs. Garashanin advised Mihailo
to do everything possible to win the Albanians over to the
Serbian side, or at least to neutralize them. Not to view
them as Turks, but to "endeavor to persuade them to
secede from the Turks." This would be no easy task, said
Garashanin, because they were dealing with people who
could neither read nor write, and who were prone to suspicion. Garashanin was fully aware of secret accomoda-
tions made by Russia and Austria with Turkey—the whole
game of "spheres of interest," and the negative role the
Albanians were assigned in that game. That is why Belgrade
diplomacy and Serbian money in the 1860s were very
active among Albanian leaders, especially the Catholics
of Northern Albania, to get them away from Italian and
Austrian influence. Five separate Albanian tribal leaders
were Garashanin's guests in Belgrade in one year.

Had Garashanin been successful, had he indeed talked
the Albanians into rebelling, would the estrangement process been turned around? Without much doubt. Had Prince
Mihailo's life dream not been brutally interrupted by an
assassin's bullet (another similarity with JFK) in 1868,
the Balkan "powder-keg" would probably have exploded
long before Albanian atrocities had gone too far to be
easily glossed over. But mistrust between the two peoples
deepened, and anti-Serbian policies of the foreign powers
were too deeply entrenched for little Serbia to handle
alone. Who knows, had the "keg" exploded some years
before Austria went into Bosnia, Hercegovina, and the
Sandjak, perhaps Bishop Njegosh and Prince Mihailo
would have ended up in Pech and Prizren respectively. And
Serbs and Albanians might have had a better chance of being friendly neighbors, at least "Balkan style."

# CHAPTER VII

## THE ALBANIANS IN THE NINETEENTH CENTURY

Albanian prospects in the Balkan constellation were not bright as 19th century events unfolded. Serbs, Greeks, Bulgarians, Montenegrins, as well as significant elements in neighboring Bosnia and Hercegovina—all were nationally fully alert, vibrating, and in some type of genuine opposition to the Turks. All of them were heading toward some form of independence and national fulfillment. And they all seemed to be gaining momentum and revelling in their fanciful dreams. It was obvious that Albania had a lot of catching up to do. Easier said than done, when one thinks of the stern Albanian reality. Albania simply could not qualify for the race. With three religions, two strikingly different mentalities (Tosk in the south and Gegh in the north), and no common alphabet literacy or written culture of their own to articulate national identity, the Albanians were not in the same class as their Hellenic and Slav competitors. With their total involvement in the passing Turkish civilization, disencumberment was practically impossible. For two reasons: they were culturally not ready for it; second, they had no cadres to do the necessary work. For the Greeks and Serbs it was a matter of renaissance. For the Albanians it was reaching for something never before experienced.

With no Hellenic past and culture to give them a sense of superiority, no medieval greatness to make them feel confident, no centuries-long resistance to feed their fortitude, Albanians found themselves in a position of a pupil totally unprepared for the forthcoming test. History was, at that time, very cruel and unfair to Albania. It pitched this small unprepared nation into combat with by far better equipped rivals. This was an unfortunate development for the future of Balkan international relations. Understandably, from the very outset Albanians were prone to panic and to paranoia. How were they going to extricate themselves from this unfavorable situation? How to prevent being "swallowed" by these foreign cultures, foreign nationalities, and strange social habits of the surrounding "small imperialists"? There was only one way, they thought, the way snails, turtles, and hedgehogs react when sensing danger: withdraw into ones shell and see an enemy in everyone and everything. Unfortunately, ever since those tantalizing days at the beginning of the 19th century, Albanians have yet to come out of that shell. This siege mentality of the past seems to explain most of the strange and peculiar behavior of Albanian individuals and society even today.

As far as the leading Albanian intellectuals were concerned, the ones that were to bring their people onto the road of national awakening, they saw Albania surrounded by three small states: Montenegro, Serbia, and Greece, which were seeking to aggrandize themselves at the expense of Albania. This frame of mind made it difficult, if not impossible, for Albania to join the other Balkan states and pull away from Turkey. On the other hand, there was no more effective way to jolt the Albanian national consciousness than by the use of such scare tactics.

Most of the protagonists of Albanian national awakening lived separated from their homeland, and were really products of foreign cultures. Such could also be said of the surrounding Greek or Slav societies. Intellectuals from the latter, however, once back, were returning to their native land which had its *own* history, culture, literacy, language, religion, and tradition—everything clearly separated from any foreign great culture. The Albanian who was returning home and wanted to begin something, to awaken his people's consciousness, had practically to create all the above enumerated. Albanians made their history in Constantinople and not in Tirana. The Albanians did not have Dushan's tsardom (as the Serbs), neither was their culture based on Hellenic civilization (as the Greeks). Albanian heroes were "Turkified outlaws," and not native mountaineers who fought for "the honorable cross and golden liberty" (as the Serbs and Montenegrins). Finally, the Albanians were not even able to write their program of national awakening in one single Albanian language common to all Albanians let alone verbalize it.

The organizational, national, and cultural obstructions that faced the Albanian patriots in the 19th century were paramount. Breaking away from Constantinople, as the source of everything good and bad that had befallen Albania, probably would not have been such a major problem, especially since that was the period when the would-be Albanian ruling class was beginning to be disenchanted with the Porte. But to induce Albanians to break away from the concept of Islamic solidarity with the Turks, or any other Moslem nation when faced by aggressive Christians, was a task of major proportions.

Typically, the realization that an attempt to break this bond was absolutely necessary came not from Albanians in the country, but from those abroad. From those Albanians who had a chance to distance themselves from the prevailing mentality at home, or who at least lived in peripheral regions of the Albanian diaspora. From those Albanians who could witness and evaluate the processes of national awakening in Italy (where a sizable Albanian minority lived), Austria, and other European countries. This, of course, made it a foreign idea, which had to be transplanted, not the genuine product of domestic soil. The American Independence idea, if born in Montreal, would not have the authenticity of the one in Philadelphia.

A considerable step was taken for the Albanians when Naum Vequiharxhi, some say a Macedonian, created an Albanian cultural organization in Romania, where he was living. In addition, by combining elements of various alphabets, he constructed a new Albanian alphabet in 1844. It was his proposed solution to one burning problem, which the Albanians did not solve until about four decades later. Vequiharxhi and others had realized that if the Albanians were ever to have a school with an Albanian teacher (not a Greek, Turk, or Italian), they first had to have an alphabet. But this obvious truth did not gain easy acceptance in the divisive conditions that were tearing Albania apart. The Albanian nation which was to be the carrier of the national ideal was yet to be formed, out of tribes of various orientations. It was therefore naive to believe that a cohesive force could be made out of something that did not exist, but Albanian patriots knew that they had to make the attempt.

For the Albanian patriots, the education of the people was a most indispensable weapon. But this was not palatable to the Turks, who in their long reign over foreign races and peoples had experienced a lot of resentment and even armed rebellion. They used force to deal with such problems, but were confused as to how to act against moves for a separate cultural identity.

With all due respect to the efforts of the Albanian patriots of that period, and to today's protagonists of the "Albanian national awakening theory," the fact remains that there was no such thing as a "national uprising" against the Turks in Albanian history. The year 1844 is usually cited as the time of numerous Albanian popular uprisings. Revolts did indeed break out in cities such as

Skoplje, Prishtina, Tetovo—none on Albanian territory proper—but these were prompted by the decision of the Turkish government to require of Albanians the same things as demanded of other Moslems in Turkey: obedience of the new military draft and the new tax laws. This terminated the special status that the Albanians had enjoyed. It takes a considerable stretching of the meaning of words to equate such opposition, undertaken in order to retain ones own privileged status, with "national awakening." Could the indignant participant in the Boston Tea Party ("no taxation without representation") be asked to liken his battle cry to the slogan that would insist on maintaining a privileged position ("representation without taxation")? By what magic twist can a fight against discrimination be equated with the struggle for the preservation of discrimination?

Albanian patriots seemingly never understood the simple truth that the only way that Albania could obtain freedom and independence was by joining hands with the Balkan Christians. This was anathema to the Moslems, but without successful Christian uprisings in the Balkans, Albanian revolts by themselves could not bring liberation. When South Albanian pashas and beys supported Turkish "pacification" of the Greek Revolution (1821), they seemingly did not know what they were doing. It seemed to them a normal Moslem cooperation, as long as the Turkish subsidies lasted. Once the money supply dried up, the Albanians rebelled. The Turkish answer: in 1830, the Turkish commander of the expeditionary force, Reshid Pasha, summoned the South Albanian leaders to Bitolj, telling them that he was bringing a "pardon" from the Sublime Porte. But on August 26th of that year, while attending a sham military parade, they were massacred, 500 of them, in a way that had nothing "sublime" about it. Albanians who survived, or heard about it, ran for cover. But where to go? To the Greeks! Similarly, in 1870 and 1910, Albanian refugees fled to Christian Cetinje.

Throughout the 19th century there were reports that Albanians were in an uproar. They revolted in 1835 (Skadar), in 1839 (Prizren), in 1844 (Skoplje, Tetovo, Prishtina), in 1845 (Prishtina), in 1847 (Sandjak of Giro-kastra). The reason for all of these rebellions was the same: the attempt of the central Turkish government to secure new income and to tighten the system of military draft. The Turks would usually begin with some kind of census, which would be a signal for the Albanians to grab their rifles. Describing the revolt of Prizren (1884), which spread to Djakovica and Prishtina, historian Stavro Skendi writes: ". . . for people who have not been used to paying taxes, or to paying very low ones, the sudden increase [in taxes] was deeply resented." (*The Albanian National Awakening*, p. 191). Usually in times of such "awakenings," the Albanian insurgents would first confront Turkish units, and the Turks would give up or postpone their demands, whereupon the Albanian rage would be turned against their Slav neighbors. The Russians would file a protest to the Sublime Porte; the Austrians and Italians would ex-press concern for the "endangered" Albanians; and the Serbs would once again try to reason with the Albanians. Every time that this game was played, the Serbs would find themselves at the shorter end of the rope.

Typical of the process were the machinations taking place in the southern areas of the old Serbian state, which toward the end of the century was also in turmoil, with Greeks, Bulgarians, Serbs, and Albanians jockeying for position. The Slavs and Greeks were in vicious competition, but they never lost sight of their enemy, the Ottoman Em-pire. Serbia, Montenegro, Bulgaria, and Greece formed an alliance, and in 1912 declared war on Turkey. The Alban-ians, on the other hand, just could not see how their inter-ests could coincide with the interests of their rivals. So, as Professor Skendi notes: "Turkey could rely on Albanians, who were hostile to Slavs. In 1901, Albanian bands pillaged and partly set fire to Novi Pazar, Sjenitsa and Prishtina.

They attacked the Slavs everywhere. The Serbian population suffered most, because of their proximity to the Albanians" (ibid., p. 201).

The Turkish administration had its reasons for keeping
the anti-Slav flame burning among the Albanians. But what
interest the Albanians had in it remains a mystery. As Turkey was about to cease being the source of power and
social advantage in the Empire, what kept the Albanians
from extending their hand to the Slavs?

All those Albanian patriots abroad, and especially those
in Constantinople, must have noticed the change in the
general attitude of the Porte toward the Serbian nation—
their visiting princes, kings, premiers, and envoys on special
missions. With Serbian rulers being received "in official
audiences at the Imperial Palace of Yildiz," would it not
have been wise to establish closer relations with the rising
crowds, and in fact "piggyback" to freedom with them?

The question must have bothered the Russian Ambassador in Constantinople, Ignatiev. He was a man of action
and even offered some of his own money (1876) for the
purpose of winning Albanians over to join the Slavs. For
the same reason, Montenegro's Prince Nikola Petrovich-
Njegosh courted the Miridite ruling family Bib Doda in the
1880s. Prince Nikola admitted that he did all this in the
hope that "when it comes to hurrah" Albanians would
join the Montenegrins in the fight against the Turks. The
Serbian government, Belgrade agents, numerous semi-offi-
cial organizations—all worked hard to attract Albanian
support for the common struggle against the Porte. They
were especially betting on a sympathetic reception among
North Albanians, whose Christian faith would prompt
them to join in fighting Islam instead of Christianity. But
this did not happen.

One such opportunity was when the Serbs of Bosnia-
Hercegovina rose up against the Turks in 1875. Serbia, although ill-prepared, came to the support of the rebels,
joined by Russian General Cherniaev and some 2,000

volunteers. Cherniaev, now a Serbian citizen, commanded the venture. Not long after, he turned tail and advised a truce, no doubt influenced by a meeting and a decision by the Russian Tsar and the Austro-Hungarian Emperor that Serbia should not be allowed to annex Bosnia. Russia sent Constantinople a strongly-worded ultimatum, while at the same time telling the Serbs to make peace.

In April 1877, however, Russia declared war against Turkey, and when she experienced tough Turkish resistance implored the Serbs to help, promising aid. The Serbs came to Russia's assistance, and by the end of December, while suffering heavy losses, forced the Turks to surrender the fortified city of Nish. Soon thereafter they ran into strong resistance at Samokovo, which was fiercely defended by Albanian troops. Forgetting promises of help to the Serbs, and the Serbs' hope of returning to Old Serbia, the Russians saw an opportunity to dictate the peace, and agreed to a truce with the Turks.

Ignoring their Serbian allies, the Russians signed the Treaty of San Stefano (March 1878), creating a Greater Bulgaria. Russia, the great "protector," did not consult her Serbian friends even unofficially. But the Serbs were not the only ones to be surprised and shocked; the Albanians were even more so. If Russia could dish out such treatment to independent Serbia, its ally, what could the Albanians, who still did not have their state and who fought on the side of the Turks, see in the cards for themselves? Not much.

The Western Great Powers, especially Austro-Hungary, realized that San Stefano meant Russian domination of the Balkans and beyond. To England and France it meant Russian control of the Straits. And Italy visualized the disastrous sight of Russian naval ships in their sea. Consequently, in less than three months, these powers called a conference at Berlin, which came to be known as the Congress of Berlin. German Chancellor Bismarck offered to be an "honest broker."

Albanian activists in Constantinople, a month before the Congress of Berlin was to meet, formed a secret "Central Committee for the Defense of the Rights of the Albanian people." It was not so secret, because several Turkish high officials of Albanian descent, were members. The Committee alleged that Serbia and other Balkan nations were desirous of annexing Albanian territories.

The Committee was the backbone in June 1878 of an Albanian assembly at Prizren, which later came to be known as the "League of Prizren." The President of the Constantinople Committee, Abdul Frasheri, delivered the opening speech in Prizren only three days before the opening of the Congress of Berlin. The largest number of Prizren participants (of a total of about 80) were from Northern Albania, and only two (including Frasheri) were from the South. Moreover, very much in attendance were Moslem landholders (some invited from Bosnia-Hercegovina), Moslem clergy, and beys and pashas—all politically conservative.

The delegates at Prizren favored the maintenance of the sovereignty of the Sultan over Albania as a guarantee against partition. As Stefanaq Pollo and Arben Puto (*The History of Albania,* Boston, 1981, p. 118) conclude: "This meant that for a while the Albanian movement and the Porte were united by common interest, for the Albanians needed the Turkish authorities to give them a free hand, and the Turks were very anxious that local resistance movements should form an obstacle to any plans to break up their empire."

The Prizren assembly drew up and sent a memorandum to the Congress of Berlin. The petition which reached the British delegation, however, was one drafted by the local committee in Skadar. It contained sentences detesting Turkish domination, a stand that the pro-Turkish conservative meeting in Prizren would not have approved. Lord Beaconsfield submitted the petition to the Congress, bringing the Albanian problem, for the first time, to the attention of international public opinion. Albanian patriots

were disappointed that in the end the Congress of Berlin
ignored the petition. The Great Powers considered Albania
still a part of Turkey, and the whole Albanian question as
constituting a Turkish internal problem.

The fact that England had assumed the role of Albania's
tutor at the Congress was not overlooked in Serbia. "At
the Congress of Berlin," wrote historian Slobodan Jovanovich, England "behaved as our enemy. The Austrian occupation of Bosnia, for example, was proposed by the English
Foreign Secretary, Lord Salisbury." ( *Vlada Milana Obreno-
vića* [Reign of Milan Obrenovich], vol. 2; Belgrade, 1927,
p. 22). One cannot help wondering if "old Slobodan" was
at all surprised when, as Premier of the Yugoslav Government in Exile, he was dumped in 1943 by Churchill in
order to create room for the ascent of Marshal Tito.

One result of the Berlin Congress was that it kindled
Albanian chauvinistic attitudes, just as San Stefano had set
afire the national intolerance of Bulgaria. In that sense,
both events only added to the existing worries of Serbia:
Turkey in the south, Austro-Hungary in the north, and now
Bulgaria in the east and Albania in the west. Territorially
and politically, both Montenegro and Serbia made modest
gains from the Berlin deliberations, which modified San
Stefano. Both were allowed some territorial expansions,
and were internationally recognized as independent states,
although de facto they had been for some time.

Turkey, which at Berlin accepted the expansions, later
resorted to delaying tactics by instigating the Albanians to
protest, and explaining to Europe that it could not ask its
Moslem troops to fight its Moslem brothers for the sake of
benefits to the Slavs. The ugliest incident in the course of
these Albanian "protests" was the killing of Mehmed Ali
Pasha, a Turkish diplomat of European renown, in
Djakovitsa on September 6, 1878. The mob dragged his
body through the streets, and paraded it with the decapitated head on a long pole. His host, the president of the
local committee of the Prizren Leage, Abdulah Pasha
Dreni, was also killed.

To most observers, the movement for Albanian national awakening had degenerated into mob rule, and the Prizren League had lost its authority over the national awakening. The Prizren League had in effect fallen into the hands of radical elements, who organized assemblies in cities such as Gjirokastra and Debar. They were routed by a Turkish expeditionary force under Dervish pasha. Abdul Frasheri was captured, sentenced to death, subsequently commuted, and finally amnestied three years later. What began as an Albanian awakening movement ended up in bands ransacking and pillaging cities and settlements, and the Turkish authorities were for the most part forced to put up with it.

Some Albanian patriots were deeply disappointed with the tactics of those who had assumed to act for the League. The unruly behavior of Northern Albanians (Geghs) horrified those in the South (Tosks). One of the Southerners was Faik Konitza, editor, author and cultured Westerner, who disapproved of violent tactics and appealed for the acceptance of civilized methods, condemning what he called "schools of assassination and massacres." Another was his close friend, Ismail Kemal Vlora, who liked to dream of a "Greco-Albanian Entente," although he was suspicious of the Greeks and especially of the Serbs. Parenthetically, it might be added that Vlora was to proclaim the first Albanian provisional govenment in 1913.

When the League of Prizren demonstrated that it was unable to guide, it meant that the Serbian side had no one to approach for a reasonable discussion. But even if there had been an Albanian representative to whom grievances could be submitted, one wonders if local Albanian "bosses" who tyrannized the Slav population could have been controlled. The situation was especially complex in the southern areas of the medieval Serbian kingdom—where three anti-Albanian groups (Serbs, Bulgars, and Greeks) were resorting to self-defense tactics.

The actions of radical Albanian elements were in part a reaction to being ignored at Berlin, together with the

realization that without Turkish help they could not prevent Serbs from eventually moving back to Old Serbia
territories. From the time of the Serbian exoduses (1690
and 1738), Albanian settlers pushed northward, taking
over more and more Serbian lands. Now, in fear and panic,
they began a migration in reverse, as they realized that the
day of reckoning might be coming. In the process, they
vented their rage on many innocent and helpless Serbs, in
some areas verging on genocide.

European capitals became concerned that the Ottoman
authorities were either unable or unwilling to put a stop to
the Albanian actions. Moscow, although sincerely moved by
the destiny of her Slav brothers in the Balkans, was prim-
arily interested in having no one to disrupt its policy in the
peninsula. Western Europeans became agitated because
they saw in all of this an excellent excuse for Moscow to
intervene. So they pressed the Ottoman Government to do
something, to go ahead with its "reform program" and to
secure a peaceful life for its Christian subjects.

Serbian envoy to Constantinople, Dr. Vladan Djordjevich, in May 1895 reported to Belgrade that he had gone
to see the Russian ambassador, to whom he complained
about Albanian atrocities, which were forcing hundreds of
families to flee to Serbia. He drew the ambassador's attention to the fact that in a relatively short period of time
the Serbs would disappear from the Kosovo vilayet. He
pointed out that those who remained in Old Serbia would
have to accept the Turkish faith in order to save their
naked lives, unless the horrible Albanian violence was
stopped.

Earlier, the ambassador told Serbia's envoy that the
situation was well known to him, because one whole village
had declared to the Russian consul that if the harassing
continued the whole village would convert to Islam. "We
will, in our hearts remain Serbs and Orthodox," the peasants declared to the consul, "but in order to save our property and our naked lives, until better times we have to

accept Islam." The ambassador promised that as soon as he had additional details, which he had requested, he would personally contact the Grand Vizier. Moreover, the ambassador agreed with the envoy's suspicion that Austria was giving encouragement and aid to the Albanians (Vladan Djordjević, *Serbija i Turska, 1894-1897;* Belgrade, 1928, p. 112).

The archbishop of the Dechani Monastery, Serafim Ristich, informed the Porte and world opinion on what was going on, by publishing *Plach Stare Srbije* (The Cry of Old Serbia), on Austrian territory (Zemun, 1864). In his memorandum to the Porte, Ristich enumerated each and every individual case of violence, terror, robbery, and outright murder performed by Albanians in the districts of Pech, Djakovitsa, Prizren, Prishtina, Novo Brdo, Gnjlane, Tetovo, Vranje, and other districts and lands. It took him 68 numbered paragraphs to describe all pertinent cases in a documented way. "Unless this savage assault on us is discontinued," wrote the archbishop, "we will be forced to leave the soil which is soaked with the blood of our ancestors, and move away from the hearths of our homes." Be it noted that this was published fourteen years before the League of Prizren which, compared to the period after the League, made the archbishop's time look relatively good.

In some ways the worst was yet to come. As the Albanian migrations in reverse continued southward, they took out their rage upon the Serbs still in Turkey. So as the century was coming to an end, and more Albanians had to migrate, more and more Serbs in Turkey were exposed to increased hatred, persecution, and mistreatment. In turn, this placed an enormous burden on Serbia: what to do to help their endangered brothers at a time when Turkish law and order were getting weaker and weaker? It is estimated that in the period 1876-1912, about 150,000 Serbs were forced to leave the Kosovo vilayet (Jovan Cvijić, *Balkanski rat i Srbija* [The Balkan War and Serbia] : Belgrade, 1912, p. 8).

# CHAPTER VIII

## PRELUDE TO WORLD WAR I:
## BALKAN WARS AND SERBO-ALBANIAN RELATIONS

The 20th century arrived with momentous events in the making or on the horizon. The Balkan peoples were in stages of uneven development. Those that had a state, such as the Serbs, were a powerful magnet for their brothers who were living under foreign rule, much to the discomfort of Austria-Hungary, which had a large Slav population within its borders. Those that did not have a state, such as the Albanians, were still attempting to begin the process of nation-building. For them, the Ottoman Empire was in the last stages of decay, but would or could the Albanians seize the opportunity to emancipate themselves?

Albanian patriots, as we saw in the previous chapter, were not able to provide adequate leadership to their nation at the time of the Prizren League and in the days that followed. There were too few of them, and they were not with their people, but outside the country. In contrast with the leaders of the Serbian uprisings, Karadjordje and Milosh, who were first among equals (a mirror image of every peasant who joined the troops), the Albanian intellectual elite that wanted to lead and was reaching out for mass support, first had to introduce themselves. The fragrance of European cities was overpowering for the sheep-herding Albanians. To the illiterate Albanian peasants, all these newcomers could have been Scandinavians, they were so remote.

The best example of this drastic remoteness is probably the author of a deeply inspired and inspiring poem, "Oh, Albania." It reads, in rough translation:

> Albanians, you are killing your brothers,
> You are divided into a hundred parties,
> Some say, I am a 'Christian';
> Others, I am a 'Moslem';
> One, I am a 'Turk'; another I am a 'Latin.'
> Still others, 'I am a Greek'; 'Slav' and others.
> But you are brothers, all of you.
> The priests and hodjas have confused you,
> Unite in one faith;
> The faith of Albanians is Albaniandom.

It was written by an Albanian Northerner from Skadar, an Albanian Christian (Catholic), Vasa Pasha Effendi, protagonist of the Latin alphabet for Albanians, and high Turkish official. The poem was published posthumously, for obvious reasons, in 1899 and in Sofia.

When the Albanian Effendi is compared with the Serb from Bosnia, Philip Vishnich, who as a child was blinded from small pox, the real difference is not in the variance of style or degree of sophistication. These two poets worked in dissimilar environments, though in the same wilderness of the Balkan mountains. One society was still dormant, the other vibrant with life. Vasa Pasha was *appealing* to his compatriots; they were misguided and not fully awake; and he himself was calling long distance. Philip, on the other hand, was at the center of events. He doggedly followed Serbia's Black George and his troops, and never ceased to *report,* to tell the story of action, of national liberation in process:

> When George ruled over Serbia,
> And baptized Serbia with the Cross,
> And took her under his wing,
> From Vidin town to the river Drina,
> From Kosovo all the way to Belgrade.

Both poems lose in translation, but both have a Homeric sound. One, however, is a product of the soil, the other of abstract intellect.

A major problem for the Albanians, in terms of national ideas, was that they were divided into three segments: those in the interior regions, those on the periphery, and those living abroad. Those in the interior were very conservative; they deeply distrusted their compatriots abroad; they believed firmly in Moslem solidarity (with the Turks); and they nursed a degree of animosity toward the Albanians who had turned Christian or who were susceptible to Latin, Slav, or Greek influences. They lived insulated in their feudal mentality, which meant that a few more decades would be needed before they would be ready for the nationalist "yeast" that was working so well in the border regions. Hence, the interior and the periphery were poles apart, while those living abroad were insistent in seeking to take the reins of the national awakening movement.

It is perhaps understandable why the Albanian patriots found it necessary to start the national "awakening" process in the border regions, where the mentality was somewhat less conservative, if not rather radical. These regions, as a rule, experienced some Greek and Slav influences. This may explain why Bitolj, Ohrid, Kichevo, Debar, Prizren, Prishtina, Djakovitsa, and Skadar attracted the "revolutionaries." There was a definite philosophical affinity between the outsiders and border region Albanians.

Turkish administration had contributed greatly to that affinity. When setting up multinational areas under their rule into "vilayets" (districts), the Turks purposely drew the dividing lines in such a way so as to encompass several nationalities in one district, instead of separating them. Whatever the rationale for such a policy, it kept rivalry alive and prevented a common front against the Turks. Using one against another, made it easier to control all of them. Were the Albanian leaders aware of this Turkish perfidy? Very much so. The first point of their national demands insisted on "Albania to be constituted as a single vilayet," meaning ethnically pure Albania. The difficulty with this was that the leaders of the Central Committee in Constantinople demanded the "union of the four vilayets of Shkodor [Skadar], Janina, Monastir [Bitolj], and Kosovo in a single pashalik governed by Albanians." But these vilayets, as drawn by Turkish administrators, included numerous Greeks, Serbs, and Bulgarians. In making such a demand, and in fighting for Skoplje, the administrative center of the Kosovo vilayet, the Albanians conveniently forgot their own earlier expressed philosophy about an ethnically pure Albanian vilayet.

To no small degree the Albanian leaders were influenced by Austria-Hungary, whose concept of a future Albania was one that Vienna intended to dominate. For the time being, however, Austria-Hungary preferred the status quo, and sought to dissuade Albanians from revolting against Turkey. They wanted Turkey intact and as strong as possible to resist Serbia. Consequently, they urged the Albanians to avoid agreements with the Slavs which were aimed against Turkey.

When in 1912, Serbia, Greece, Montenegro, and Bulgaria declared war on Turkey, neither Austria nor the Albanians were ready for the Balkan blitz. Certain Serbian emissaries had talked with some Albanian leaders, exploring the possibilities of joining in an insurgency against the Turks. But the Albanians could not at that time fathom the military weaknesses of the Turkish army, so they stayed aloof.

Moreover, there was as yet no unity among the Albanian leaders, no common point of view. Most of them were against the Young Turks, but not Turkey. And when the

Young Turks consented not to push reforms, Albanian animosity mollified. The Serbs were still regarded as the common enemy, "giaurs," to whom the Young Turks had wanted to entrust "police duties" in settlements of mixed ethnicity! For the Albanians that was utter madness, and they just could not take it. They could not see a "Sultan's sabre dangling from a giaur's hip," particularly since the Albanians had such a low opinion of Serbian arms. This low opinion of Serbian arms was influenced by what Austria-Hungary told them. Secondly, the Turks certainly were not about to admit how weak they were. Thirdly, Albanian unrestricted violence against the defenseless Serbian population in Kosovo and elsewhere, in the period 1903-1912, had made them overconfident.

Albanian violence in those years seemed to know no bounds. When George Stepanovich Scherbin was allowed by the Turkish government to open the Russian Consulate in Kosovska Mitrovitsa, local Albanians, led by Isa Boletini, decided that they could not be. They besieged the city (March 1903), and were repulsed by the Turkish garrison. Ten days later, however, the Consul was assassinated. Albanians considered him guilty for the fact that the time had come for "Moslems to make way for Christians." The Albanians also attacked the town of Vuchitrn, ransacked the Serbian Church, "searching for arms." And they swarmed into the city of Kolashin, closing schools, expelling Serbian teachers, and "looking for rifles," allegedly smuggled in from Serbia. Serbian consuls in the area were sending back reports that sounded like real horror stories, and the Serbian Premier, Nikola Pashich, deplored the "difficult situation facing the Serbs in the area." Turkish authorities were either unable or unwilling to stop the Albanian harassment of Serbs.

When informed of rumors about an assault of Albanians on Prizren, many local Turks began packing and heading south for safer cities. Everything pointed to total chaos, which culminated in the massive march of some 15,000

Albanians on Skoplje (August 12, 1912). Even when earlier
Sultan Mehmed V himself came to Kosovo, Albanians, en-
raged by the Turkish reforms, were not listening anymore.
Armed Albanian units occupied Djakovitsa, Mitrovitsa,
and finally entered Skoplje. And Turkey, in a state of political transition, felt that action against the Albanian insurgents could wait.

In the meantime, the Balkan powers had moved swiftly
in their war against the Ottoman Empire. The Serbs defeated the Turks at Kumanovo (October 23, 1912), and
met with the Montenegrin forces in Metohija (October
29). The Montenegrins liberated Pech and Djakovitsa,
while the Serbian army entered Prishtina and Prizren.
Kosovo was free! And one of Vienna's prime aims in the
Balkans, the prevention of a common border between
Serbia and Montenegro had been nullified.

When Serbia realized that there was an opportunity to
reach the sea, the army was ordered to cross the river Drim.
It pushed through Albania, entering the cities of Ljesh,
Kroja, and Tirana. On November 29th the Serbian cavalry
waded into the Adriatic, and took the port of Drach. The
Albanians, during this sweep, fought in the ranks of the
Turkish army. As the situation at the front worsened, how-
ever, they started to trickle off and desert.

Europe gasped in disbelief! As the news from the front
began reaching the capital cities, the Great Powers were
surprised, but Vienna was stunned. The German General
Staff took it as a personal humiliation, because the Turkish
officers were practically their pupils. The "Drang nach
Osten" was jeopardized. Franz Ferdinand, at one gala
soupee in Vienna called the Serbs "a bunch of thieves,
murderers, no-goods, and hooligans," as Vienna was pre-
paring for a diplomatic denial of Serbia's achievements.
The Russians, who until recently had seriously objected
to Serbian impatience, now were elated. Foreign Minister
Sazonov told the Serbian envoy in St. Petersburg: "Now,
you will see, I will be your best lawyer!" British diplomat,

George Buchanan, however, when told of the Serbian army being in Drach, remarked sarcastically to the Serbian minister: "Oh, you already have a name for Durazzo."

Albanian nationalist leaders were in shock. Stvaro Skendi says that: "the problem which the patriots had to face was very grave: the fate of their country." (*The Albanian National Awakening,* p. 451). He emphasizes that the situation was even more "entangled" by the lack of central authority that all Albanians would recognize, and by the disruption of communications. "Albanians fought on the side of Turkey because they believed that by doing so they would best safeguard their own territory" (ibid., p. 452). Now they were seeing Montenegro besieging Skadar in the North, the Serbian forces occupying the heart of Albania, and Greeks marching to Janina. They were witnessing what they had always feared most: the "dismemberment of Albania."

Top leaders among Albanian nationalists (Ismail Kemal, Faik Konitza, Fan Noli, and others) were caught unprepared for the Turkish defeat. Overnight all Albanian eyes turned toward Vienna, the only possible savior by virtue of the diplomatic and military power it could wield. Vienna became the mecca for Albanian nationalists, and Sami bey Frasheri in 1913 published (in Vienna and Leipzig) the German translation of his book, *Was war Albanien, was is es, was wird es werden?* (cited earlier).

On his way to Albania from Constantinople, Ismail Kemal, in addition to visiting other cities, stopped in Budapest. There he met Count Leopold Berchtold, Austro-Hungary's foreign minister. On the basis of talks in Budapest and prior to that in Vienna, Ismail Kemal felt confident enough to cable his son in Vlore (Albania): "Avenir Albanie assure." One month after leaving Constantinople, Ismail Kemal arrived at Drach (November 21, 1912), on a boat placed at his disposal by Berchtold. He got out of the city in the nick of time, on the way to his hometown of Vlore, not to witness the arrival of the Serbian army

(November 29). He was not welcomed as warmly in Drach as he would be in his home town. Landowning beys were opposed to him, and many citizens still preferred to view the Turkish flag instead of the Albanian one. But in Vlore, where about 80 delegates from all over Albania assembled, things went smoothly for the proclamation of Albanian independence and the formation of a provisional government. Vienna's foreign minister had emphasized that at that critical moment the image of unity among the Albanians had to be maintained, if Vienna's role of defending Albania and stopping Serbia was to succeed on the diplomatic front.

In the meantime, the Serbo-Montenegrin occupation of Northern Albania became a topic of international concern. The London Conference of Ambassadors was called (December 17, 1912), to decide on Albanian frontiers, and on the withdrawal of the occupation forces. The future of the victorious Serbian exploit did not seem bright. Austria-Hungary, which had been surprised by the Balkan powers' swift action, was adamant. It insisted on a Serbian pullout, and the creation of a separate Albanian unit. It appeared that Vienna was looking for a *casus belli*. The Great Powers took it seriously, and began pressing Serbia to give in. The Serbian position was that they had fought against Turkey (the powers had always maintained that this was Turkish territory), and they would not budge until peace talks had been concluded. Deep in their heart, they knew that this was bravado. One by one, Serbia's "friends" advised a pullout. Britain, France, and finally Russia, told Serbia that they would not risk a European war for some small cities in the Balkan peninsula.

Sazonov, who had earlier promised Serbia that he would be her "best lawyer," warned the Serbian envoy in St. Petersburg: "Watch out. Don't insist on Drach, because you might lose Belgrade. Vienna has lost its head." (Dimitrije Popović, *Borba za narodno ujdinjenje, 1908-1914* [Struggle for National Unification]; Belgrade, 1936, p.

100). Serbia could not be satisfied with such brotherly
advice.When Serbia's prime minister, Nikola Pashich, asked
what they should do in the face of Austrian intransigence,
Sazonov replied: "We are ready to defend the political
and economic emancipation of Serbia and its exit to the
sea across Albanian territory [meaning free transit] . . .
and to work for the drawing of Serbo-Albanian borders as
much to the West as possible. But we do not believe that
Serbia will be given a sovereign right at any point on the
Adriatic coast. . . . Imperial Russia must be sure that
Serbia will accept the decision arrived at by the Great
Powers. Otherwise, Serbia cannot count on our support,
and in that case neither England nor France will help
Serbia. Neither Russia nor her allied powers can allow the
question of European war to be decided by Serbia." (Ibid.,
p. 102.)

Pashich's government replied: ". . . With great sacrifices,
Serbia has liberated Serbs from the Turks, and reached the
littoral which once belonged to her. . . . However, in view
of the desires of Austria, which has declared that it cannot
agree with the Serbian retention of the littoral, taken by
arms . . . the Serbian Government . . . entrusts to the Great
Powers the solution of the Serbian outlet to the Adriatic
sea." (Ibid., p. 103.)

The Conference of Ambassadors decided on the "creation
of an autonomous Albania, under the sovereignty and
suzerainty of the Sultan, and under the exclusive guarantee
of the six Great Powers. Serbia will be reserved a commercial outlet to one Albanian port, free and neutral . . . for
all commodities, including munitions." But Vienna balked
at this proposition and increased its military preparedness.

In the meantime, a new inflamatory point emerged, the
question of Skadar, besieged by the Montenegrins. King
Nikola wanted it badly, but he had no heavy artillery. Essad Pasha defended it ably. After five months, however, he
surrendered the city to jubilant Montenegrins (April 23,
1913). Only a week later, the Great Powers on Orthodox

Easter Sunday demanded that King Nikola withdraw his
troops. Vienna and the Vatican insisted that Skadar not
be given to Montenegro, and the former stepped up its
mobilization.

Serbia had already agreed to pull out its troops "once
peace is signed and related questions settled," and advised
Montenegro to do the same. Nikola Pashich of Serbia told
King Nikola of Montenegro: "The sacrifice is difficult, but
it must be borne when the whole of Europe demands it."
And Tsar Nikola of Russia advised the same thing. Nikola,
the king of Montenegro, did not believe it, when from his
mountain view of the sea, he observed an international
naval force (Austria-Hungary, France, and England) poised
in the blue waters.

Peace with Turkey was signed on May 30, 1913, and the
withdrawal of occupying Serbian troops began, mostly via
the sea route, through Salonika. In the meantime, the
Greeks and the Serbs had agreed on their respective spheres
of interest in Albania (South and North of the river
Shkombra). The Serbian army retained strategic positions
in the border belt, and dug in. This offered an ideal opportunity for Albanian guerrillas to prolong the bellicose
situation, and in September 1913, massively attacked the
cities of Debar and Struga. When Serbian reinforcements
drove them out of the cities a month later, the Serbian
army crossed the river Drim and invaded the regions of
Mati and Malesia. It was a militarily tactical move, but the
European Powers immediately branded it "another Serbian
drive toward the Albanian littoral."

To the Austrians, the behavior of Serbia was unfathomable. Accustomed, in its imperial haughtiness, in manipu-
lating the "civilized" Slavs of its own multi-national state,
Vienna just did not know how to handle the "Balkanese."
The confrontation more and more took on a David-and-
Goliath aspect, and the old empire was uncomfortable with
that image. Just as Vienna thought it had won the second
round (the first being the Serbian entry into Albania), the

bloody Serbs were again in Albania. When the Serbs occupied Albanian territory for the second time, Austria-
Hungary sent an ultimatum to Belgrade, requesting a pull
out within eight days. On the advice of Russia, Serbia
gave in.

Yet the very existence of Serbia grated on the Austrian
nerve. The nation which at the time of the Congress of
Berlin had a population of under two million, now had
four and one half million, with its territory doubled.
Serbia needed a commercial outlet to the sea (Salonika
or an Adriatic port), but Austria would not hear of it.
Vienna insisted on controlling the external trade of Serbia,
by routing it through its own (Austrian) territory. This is
what Pashich called a "stranglehold." How long would
David be able to keep his cool in front of Goliath's constant bullying? David had just repulsed another attempt to
push him around—the Bulgarian troops that crossed Serbia's
frontier in 1913, were badly beaten by the Serbs. Once
again, Vienna felt humiliated by this nation of "peasants"
and "palace murderers," a reference to the assassination of
Serbia's King, Alexander Obrenovich, in 1903.

Austria-Hungary was waiting for an opportunity to
strike, and Nikola Pashich could sense it. He knew that
Vienna would not desist from bullying Serbia. In St. Peters-
burg, in the early spring of 1914, he conveyed his fears to
Tsar Nicholas II. Pashich knew that a preventive war against
Serbia had become a necessity for the rulers in Vienna.
Nicholas was disbelieving, but promised help in case of an
unprovoked attack on Serbia.

But, in the end, what became of the Albanian minuet?
The Conference of Ambassadors, which first decided to give
Albania an autonomous status within Turkey, later qualified its recommendations, since the Turks had agreed to
pull out from the western regions of the Balkan peninsula.
In the spring of 1913, "independence" was substituted for
"autonomy," and Austria-Hungary and Italy were entrust-
ed with the task of working it out. By the end of July

1913, the ambassadors finally decided it would need a body of "six plus one" (six representatives of the Great Powers and one Albanian) to set up the new administration. German Prince Wilhelm von Wied was chosen to become "hereditary Prince of Albania." He did not stay long enough to get to know his subjects. He left in a hurry, as soon as he learned that the Archduke was felled by a shot of a young Serbian nationalist, an Austro-Hungarian subject and on Austro-Hungarian territory (Sarajevo).

A great deal of squabbling, tense dispute, and hard driving give-and-take took place during the months (1913) of the London ambassadorial meetings. The participants agonized over the death of Turkey, the birth of Albania, and the demands of the Balkan allies. Serbia and Montenegro sent to London the cream of their diplomatic corps (Stojan Novakovich, Andra Nikolich, and Milenko Vesnich for Serbia, and Lazar Mijushkovich for Montenegro). Neither the Serbs nor the Montenegrins worried too much about the question of the form of the Albanian state or its status. As far as they were concerned, creating an independent state in their immediate neighborhood was a blessing. It was always better to have a small, hopefully reasonable, nation at your border than an insatiable imperialistic Great Power, be it Italy, Turkey, or Austro-Hungary. The main concern of the Serbs were the boundary lines, and a convenient outlet to the sea. When it became clear that they would be deprived of the latter, the Serbian team concentrated on the boundary line.

As far as the Albanians were concerned, one would have expected that of the three items on their agenda, national independence, domestic system, and frontiers, the last would have the lowest priority. But this was not the case. The most "awakened" among the "awakened" Albanians were from the border areas. If they had to choose between living in Slav Serbia or Moslem Turkey, they would always opt for Turkey. In what form, system, or arrangement was of secondary importance. It was a totally reverse line of thinking, as compared to the Serbian one. When one century earlier, Milosh was in their situation, he first grabbed whatever form of national assertion was possible, leaving geography to worry about later.

Evaluating the ambassadorial decision of July 29, 1913, regarding Albania, one cannot avoid a feeling of pity and sorrow. It was a profoundly meaningless turn in the history of the Albanian people: politically the Turkish ruler was replaced by a German prince; socially the feudal system was taken over by the westernized offspring of former lords; culturally, they were subject to a non-Moslem culture; and nationally, they became an appendage of the Vienna foreign office. Was all that less important than who would get the city of Djakovitsa?

By concentrating on the question of frontiers, the Albanians badly hurt themselves. First, they had to go through a humiliating lecturing that the principle of "national borders" could not be applied to a non-existing state (the Russians harped on that). Second, what they claimed to be "Albanian" was in fact Turkish territory (the Serbs harped on that). Third, they had to throw themselves completely into the lap of Christian Vienna, without being able to preserve even the smallest independent action. And fourth, which was the most important, they did not get a single border town that they had asked for. Even Skadar was finally occupied by a British admiral, who placed the town under the control of an international force, and not the "Albanian" government in Vlore.

What the Albanian leaders never understood was that just as Russia or Britain would not risk a war for Debar, neither would Vienna. Logically, boundary problems should have been the subject of discussion among those most directly concerned, Serbia and Albania. Essad Pasha, the defender of Skadar, was one of the few Albanians who understood that. But the Albanian leaders in Vlore expelled him from the country for such thoughts. In their opinion he was a traitor. Of all people, the man who prevented Montenegro

from incorporating Skadar, became an Albanian "traitor"!
Essad Pasha, after his expulsion went to Nish, which was
at that time the seat of the Serbian government. Essad
Pasha's ideas of returning to his country (already in a
stage of civil war), and establishing his own authority,
and even proclaiming himself ruler, met with the full support of the Serbs. He formed his own government in Drach
in September 1914. But by that time nobody could save
Albania. The Italians were in the port of Vlore (Valona),
and on the island of Saseno, and, as World War I came,
Bulgarian and Austro-Hungarian armies occupied most of
Albania.

In Cetinje, the impervious and durable ruler of Montenegro, King Nikola, the "European father-in-law" as he
was known, could never forgive Europe for taking Skadar
away from him. Montenegrins were always proud of being
Serbs, and rejoiced in every Serbian success. When in 1913
the Bulgarians broke away from the Balkan alliance and
attacked Serbia, Montenegrins came 12,000 strong to help
the Serbian army. At the end of the Balkan wars, however,
there was in their Serbian bosom a certain envy. They saw
that the Serbs got their Prizren, but that Montengro did
not get its Skadar. They saw the Serbs as jubilant, and
themselves in mourning. The two brothers felt differently
about the war that they had fought together and the outcome that they shared.

In a sense, the war was misdirected. When Serbia's leaders talked about an outlet to "the coast that had been
ours before," they were referring to the estuary of the
Neretva river and the littoral south of it. At that time,
however, Austria-Hungary was in Bosnia-Hercegovina and
in the bay of Kotor. Consequently, the entry of Serbian
forces in those areas would have meant war with Vienna.
Serbia and Montenegro tried to compensate in Turkish Albania. Vienna had no qualms about occupying Serbian
lands, but it could not tolerate Slavs in Albanian lands.

Before the curtain fell on Serbia and Montenegro, the two small brothers showed the world what hearts beat in them. On July 28, 1914, Austria-Hungary declared war on Serbia. Old Pashich was eating his lunch in a local pub when the courier brought him the sealed envelope. His only comment to a bystander was: "This is the end of Austria. Lord Almighty will help us to come out winners." Finally, the Chief of the Austro-Hungarian General Staff, Conrad, had his way: he had asked for war on Serbia some twenty times!

According to Vienna's envoy at the Vatican, the latter approved of the war. The Vatican Secretary of State, Del Val, told Vienna's Palfi: ". . . let us hope the Monarchy will finish the task it started, and destroy Serbia." (Vladimir Dedijer in Bozich, Ivan, et al., *Istorija Jugoslavije* [History of Yugoslavia] : 2nd ed., Belgrade, 1973, p. 383).

The Austro-Hungarian commander on the Balkan front, General Potiorek, moved his invading army through Bosnia, attacking Serbia on the flank, hoping to occupy most of it in two to three weeks. After a few initial skirmishes and withdrawals, the Serbs stood up at chosen positions and routed Potiorek's army across the Sava river, recapturing occupied Belgrade. Again, Central Europe was stunned, Russia elated, Western Europe pleasantly surprised. Potiorek was demoted. Humiliated Vienna in 1915 watched as German commander, General Mackensen, the winner of the battle of Gerlitz (against the Russians earlier in the year), took over. His Prussian General Staff drew up plans that would make possible for a German motorized division to surround the army of Balkan peasants. Three times the Germans tried, three times the peasants, low on munitions and rations, outmaneuvered them, and finally withdrew to their destiny-determining Kosovo. The Bulgarian army, in a sneak stab in the back in October, closed the retreat route toward Greece. A French task force in Greece was told to abandon rescue operations. The only way out for the Serbian forces was through the mountains of Montenegro and Albania.

This time the flesh hungry Kosovo soil would receive only cold heavy guns and armament, while the "skeletons" would head to the snow-covered mountain passes. There the Albanian sharpshooters would be waiting for them, although Essad Pasha's friendship with Pashich to a degree eased the Serbian retreat. At the head of the retreating Serbian Army, peasant-soldiers carried four lighted candles, protecting the flames from the mountain winds, and one sarcophagus. They were moving the bones of Serbia's king, Stefan the First-Crowned, lest they be desecrated either by Bosnian Moslems in the Austro-Hungarian army or by the "liberated" Albanians from Kosovo. Stefan was used to such escapades; he must have gone through twenty of these in the five centuries of Serbian history. The coffin was finally laid to rest in Montenegro's Ostrog Monastery.

Montenegro was not to remain free either. The mountain people repulsed at the battle of Mojkovats several Austrian attempts to intercept the Serbian retreat to the sea. One third of the 400,000 Serbs who met Mackensen on the Danube made it to the coast, to re-emerge on the Salonika front in 1916. Montenegrins fought as long as they could, then offered peace talks. The angry Austrians demanded unconditional capitulation, including the delivery of the passing Serbian "skeletons." To surrender their own ragged, emaciated, and half-frozen brothers to the hated enemy was inconceivable. Instead King Nikola and his premier left Montenegro—no truce, no capitulation, no signed instrument. The Austrians entered Montenegro as ignored occupiers. The state of war with Montenegro was never formally terminated. There is disagreement among Yugoslav historians, however, as to whether some form of surrender instrument was signed by Montenegrin military commanders.

# CHAPTER IX

## WORLD WAR I AND
## NEW TUTELAGE FOR ALBANIA

As the end of World War I approached, and Serbia inched ever nearer to the fulfillment of its war aim—the unification of all South Slavs in one independent state—relations with Albanians took a new turn. The mighty Albanian protector, and the main instigator of anti-Serbian attitudes in the area, Austria-Hungary, was about to leave the historical scene. That was the good news. The bad news was that it was about to be replaced by Italy, which during the war had settled Albanians in Serbian areas, certainly not a friendly act. Moreover, Italy had the support of the West, which Vienna did not. The Entente had made numerous promises to Italy in the Secret Treaty of London (1915), and Italy wasted no time in seeking to cash in.

But Italian and Serbian (Yugoslav) claims to former Austro-Hungarian territories overlapped. Serbia wanted Skadar, as a natural part of Montenegro, the real hinterland of the city. Montenegrins had spilled so much blood for it in the recent past, in vain. The new government in Belgrade wanted a degree of influence in Albania, especially in the northern part, and a few frontier "corrections."

112

In general, Belgrade could live with the borderline drawn by the 1913 London Conference. Also, as it turned out, Yugoslavia was among the few voices among the allies pleading for an independent Albania, free of any Great Power patronage.

The Serbian (Yugoslav) position was markedly different from the Italian. The disparity was not only with respect to territorial demands and ambitions, but mainly in the conceptual aspect of the demands. Italy, which had begun with an interest in the Albanian littoral, now wanted half of Albania, and was pushing the Great Albania concept, which meant the incorporation of Serbian lands, such as Kosovo, into the new Albanian state. There was no way that such a proposal would be acceptable to a nation that had just come out of the war a winner.

Belgrade's position on Kosovo was not negotiable, and had not changed one iota since the discussions at the London Conference of Ambassadors (January 1913). First Serbia could not allow the Kosovo area to be a "malignant tumor" that would bleed Serbia's state power. Second, Serbia never considered Kosovo as "small change" or a "bargaining chip" to be used by diplomats at the bargaining table. Third, the Serbs could have used the right of conquest argument, since the Turks had conquered it from them, but chose not to do so. Rather, they stressed Serbia's historic, cultural, and moral rights.

The historic, cultural, and moral reasons which guided Belgrade in opposing foreign pretentions to Kosovo were fully presented to the London meeting in 1913, and did not change in 1919 in the Royal Yugoslav format, and are just as valid today, some sixty years later, although in a diametrically different ideological context.

The memorandum submitted by Serbia's delegates to the 1913 conference, read in part:

> Today the majority in those areas are Arnauts [Albanians], but from the middle of the 14th century until the end of the

17th century that land was *so pure Serbian* . . . that the Serbs
established their Patriarchate in Pech . . . and near Pech is the
Serbian monastery, Dechani, the most famous monument of
Serbian architecture and piety from the 14th century. It is
impossible to imagine that [these] would have been built in a
region in which the Serbian people was not in a majority. The
region in which are found Pech, Djakovitsa, and Dechani, is
the most holy among all Serbian lands. It is impossible to
imagine any Montenegrin or Serbian government which would
be in a position to yield that land to Arnauts or to any one
else . . . . On that question the Serbian people cannot and will
not yield, nor enter into any agreements or compromises, and
therefore the Serbian government is not in a position to do
so . . . .

One cannot over-emphasize the moral impact that the
liberation of Kosovo (cradle of the nation) had as a fulfillment of Serbia's historic mission. Rational Western diplomats had difficulty understanding this. Operating in
societies where traditional values are, if necessary, also
negotiable, they viewed Serbia's history in terms of "progress" made in a brief span of time. They could not understand the uncompromising position of the Serbs when it
came to losing a few cities here and there, compared to the
overall national advantage gained in only a few years. The
"some you lose, some you win" philosophy could not be
applied to Kosovo. Serbia just could not accept the Entente's concept of giving certain Serbian lands to Serbia in
exchange for giving other equally historic Serbian lands to
someone else.

European diplomatic big guns like Lloyd George (who
in 1919 said, "I've got to polish off Pashich") or Izvolski
(who once called Pashich, "this old conspirator"), as well
as British public opinion moulders such as Wickham Steed
and R. W. Seton-Watson, were plainly annoyed with Serbia's stubborness. The latter twosome envisioned the new
state of the South Slavs in terms of a Central Europe constellation. They feared Serbian "hegemonism" and fell
for Italian scare tactics, portraying the Slav monster as

"stretching from Vladivostok to the Adriatic." To them, the fact that Tsar Dushan (1331-1354) had one of his palaces adjacent to Skadar; that that city was the capital of the Montenegrin ruling family of Chrnojevich (1465-1490); that the widow of Serbia's King Urosh ( (1242-1276) built her monastery there and lived there as a nun; that Skadar had a Serbian school as late as 1850; that the city was ecclesiastically part of the Prizren Orthodox diocese until 1913—all this meant nothing, or very little.

Once again the Serbs had an image problem in Western Europe. Again the British Foreign Office had suspicions regarding Serbian motives. Serbian historian Milorad Ek-mechich writes: "The Serbian Government could not get rid of the burden which history has placed upon her shoulders—the prejudice in Western Europe about the historic mission of Serbia, which is to open the door to the Russians in the South of Europe. . . . Britain viewed Serbia exclusively from that perspective." (*Ratni ciljevi Srbije 1914* [War Aims of Serbia]; Belgrade, 1973, p. 437).

Two Albanian authors, Stefanaq Pollo and Arben Puto (*The History of Albania,* London, 1981, p. 182), assert that there were other considerations. In explaining the admission of Albania to the League of Nations in 1920, they write:

> The unexpected interest in the Albanian cause on the part of London was not unconnected with the petroleum wealth to be found in the Albanian subsoil. . . . The Foreign Office told the Tirane Government that it could count on Britain's firm support if it allowed the Anglo-Persian Company exclusive rights to prospect and exploit the petroleum resources in Albania. The Government accepted [the offer] and so, on December 17, the British representative, H. A. L. Fisher, declared to the General Assembly that his delegation had undertaken "a new and thorough study of the Albanian situation" which has convinced it that Albania should be admitted immediately.

The validity of this contention is beyond the scope of this study, but suffice it to say that Britain did on different occasions support Albanian positions against Belgrade. Moreover in 1921, Britain was influential in the Conference of Ambassadors (this time in Paris), which in addition to deciding on the borders of the new state, resolved that the territorial integrity of the Albanian state to be a matter of "international interest." Consequently, it was agreed that Italy was to be endowed with the "protection" of Albania within the League of Nations system. This meant giving Italy a hand in Albanian internal affairs, which seemed to put Belgrade on notice of Italian intentions in the Balkans.

Serbian Premier Nikola Pashich had something to say about United States attitudes toward Serbia in those days. He had nothing against Wilson's fourteen points or his steadfast defense of the right of self-determination. But he felt that there was a flaw in Wilson's personal insistence on Albania's "independent" status. In the view of the season-ed Serbian politician, an "independent Albania" under an Italian "protectorate" was a contradiction in terms. Pash-ich believed that it would have been more logical to have the two states, Serbia (Yugoslavia) and Albania, cooperate in defending the Balkan area against intrusions of foreign influences of all kinds. In one report to the National As-sembly, Pashich declared that on the one hand, Wilson "protects Albania from us,and on the other hand, he brings Italy into Albania, the most dangerous enemy not only of the Albanian people, but of the whole Balkan pen-insula as well."

In this "exit Austria—enter Italy" scenario, Pashich saw the opposite of freedom from foreign intervention in Balkan affairs. In the multinational environment of the Balkans, ethnic tensions and national conflicts were not to be dreaded as much—he thought—as the exploitation of those tensions and rivalries by a foreign power. Even if one attempted to understand the concern of the Entente

(and the United States) about maintenance of peace in the
Balkans, to appoint Italy to be the protector of Albania
and, indirectly, the guardian of the peace in the area, was
equal to assigning a fox as caretaker of the chicken coop,
as events in the 1930s were to demonstrate.

# CHAPTER X

## BETWEEN TWO WORLD WARS

When in early 1920, some 450,000 Schipetars, living mostly in the Kosovo-Metohija region, looked to Belgrade for help and guidance in adjusting to their new status in the family of Slavs, they did not realize how little aid the new Kingdom of the Serbs, Croats, and Slovenes could give, because the entire country was in dire straits. Moreover, the task of organizing the newly created state was enormous. Leadership fell largely to Serbia, which had spearheaded the unification movement. But to move from the homogeneous Serbian state to one of considerable diversity, and four times larger in geographic size, with all the other problems associated with building a new nation, constituted a challenge never before faced.

Understandably, with so many problems of greater urgency, some normal for a war-ravaged country and others new and unanticipated, the central government did not give the Albanian plight a high priority. There were two tasks that seemed rather logical: first, the badly needed re-Serbianization of Kosovo, justified by centuries' long effort by a foreign occupier to denationalize it. The most suitable way to do it was through abolishing semi-feudal economic conditions that prevailed in the area, which meant going ahead with agrarian reforms that had long been overdue under the Turks. The second imminent task was to bring the Albanian masses into the modern political process, which had existed in Serbia and was about to begin functioning in the new state. This task was left to the existing political parties, most logically to those of Serbia, but those in other parts of the country were also free to enter the political arena.

Albanian Schipetars or Arnauts, as they were called, were in much deeper difficulties than Belgrade ever realized. First, they were a closed society; new ideas could not easily penetrate. Secondly, the bitter taste of what Albanians had done in the past, influenced the Serbs to keep their distance and to refuse to get involved in the "salvation" of the Albanian minority. Third, the resistance of local "katchaks" was highly visible, as well as the activity of Kosovo Albanians in exile. Last, but not least, the broad masses of the Schipetars in the Kingdom of the Serbs, Croats, and Slovenes were existing on a very low economic level. With no schooling at all, they were totally dependent for leadership on local hodjas and Moslem overlords. It was impossible to find Schipetar teachers (Albania itself could not provide them), let alone capable administrators, trained policemen, or professionals (doctors, engineers, et al.). Sending a Serbian teacher into an Albanian village meant forcing a Schipetar father to decide whether he would let the Orthodox teacher or the Moslem hodja educate his son, and whether he would give up the custom of not sending the female child to school.

The pressures were enormous, really overwhelming, for the impoverished and uneducated Schipetar. The cultural barrier began to crack only later, when local boys had a chance to serve their military term in the new army, where they were exposed to modern ways of life and learned to read and write.

Belgrade accepted the stipulations of the Treaty of St. Germain (1920) concerning the protection of national minorities. These included all the great sounding principles of equality before the law, political rights, civil rights, usage of the mother tongue, right to public instruction, religious guarantees, etc. In principle, these sounded great, but how much of scarce resources was the new state obliged to allocate in an effort to achieve all of these aspirations?

The new government was not a wealthy uncle, and Serbia proper (along with Montenegro) was the hardest hit part of the new nation by the devastations of two Balkan wars and World War I. The ideological South Slav euphoria had a very meager material base, which was very much disoriented at that. It was nice to proclaim a principle and design a program, but when it came to realizing it, the Serbian colonists, the ones who were brought to Kosovo to "re-Serbianize" it, were the most vocal victims of that reality. The problem had nothing to do with nationalism. The state had to make due; there was no UNRRA or other relief agency, and the Hoover European Rehabilitation program concentrated mainly on Belgium.

The insufficient response to the problems of Kosovo and Methoija, whatever the reasons, undoubtedly opened up an opportunity for anti-state (mainly anti-Serb) elements in the area to fan the flames of disappointment. As the armed but spotty opposition to the new state was dying out, and life seemed to return to a type of normalcy, the Kosovo program, if it can be called that, was mainly visible through the work of the Special Commission whose task was to redistribute the lands obtained in the agrarian reform. It is estimated that about 60,000 Serbs from Bosnia, Hercegovina, Lika, and Montenegro homesteaded in the region, through the work of this commission. It was a frustrating task and a tiresome process, consuming great energy, time and cost, mainly because there were no reliable documents to work with. The land that had belonged to the former spahis and beys had no deeds, and some of this property was claimed by many families and institutions (churches, cooperatives, clans, and tribes) as "usurped" in the past. There were lands belonging to "outlaws" hiding in the woods or who had crossed over into Albania. There were properties so atomized and dispersed that it was impossible to put them together. There were pieces of land that nobody claimed, or that the spahis were not even aware that they owned them.

Most of the land available for homesteading belonged to Turks who had left with the Turkish army, or who had moved to Asia Minor. Some of this migration continued until the late 1930s. About 40,000 Turks left Kosovo and other South Serbian regions, and many from Bosnia as well. Another 40,000 were Albanians who, being Moslems, declared themselves Turks. The official policy of the Belgrade government was to encourage Turks and Albanians to leave. In the process there were some injustices and abuses, but this was not the intention of the law. Cases of over-reaction, revenge, and misuse of authority were reported, but they were a far cry from the situation which existed at the beginning of the century, when the Serbian population was terrorized by the Albanians on the loose, with no strong government authority to stop them. In general, it can be said that after 1918 there was no revenge on the part of Serbia against Turks or Albanians because of their misdeeds against the Serbs throughout the centuries.

One lesson that the members of the anti-Yugoslav Kosovo Committee in exile, and local Albanian outlaws, learned was that the Yugoslav army and gendarmerie would not tolerate Albanian excesses as had the Turks. Belgrade could not be blackmailed as Constantinople had been. Attacks on frontier posts or individual terrorists acts against the police or other authorities were harshly dealt with, and those giving sanctuary to guerrillas were severely punished if they could be located.

All of this had some unfortunate consequences: first, it prevented the normal integration of Albanians into the social life of the new state; second, it antagonized the central government to which Albanians had been turning for help; third, it hurt,primarily and most of all, those among the Albanian population who needed help most.

One should note that Serbs from Serbia itself were the least interested in settling in Kosovo, or of profiting from the opportunity. Those who came to Kosovo were Serbs from other areas. Inhabitants of Serbia proper never cast their eyes on neighboring lands, because they had no need for them. This is why a Serbian peasant is still sincerely taken aback when he hears anyone accusing him of "hegemonism." Of all those Serbian peasants in army uniform who roamed the vast latifundias of liberated South Serbia, Bosnia, Croatia, and Slovenia—not a single one stayed there after his release from the army. Neither did any one of them show any desire to settle there. They were startled by the number of landless farm laborers in all those regions, and felt good about helping them to become landowners, providing them an opportunity freely to exercise their political and civil rights. All this, only to hear them, a few years down the road, accused of "Serbian hegemonism."

What happened in Kosovo after World War I was not just a "change of occupiers," the Serbian master replacing the Turkish one, as some circles like to portray it. The fact is that after centuries of social immobility, Kosovo suddenly went through a revolutionary change. The Serbian liberation of Kosovo, in a small way, resembled the Napoleonic push through Europe. It opened many doors to the Albanians. That they were unable or unwilling to use them is another matter.

One of the most unfortunate things for the Albanian masses of Kosovo was their being abandoned by their leaders. As if that was not enough, these same leaders instigated Kosovo Schipetars to act against the Yugoslav authorities. The mushrooming of "committees for the liberation of Kosovo," in Albania and elsewhere, resulted in the sending of terrorists and irredenta literature into the Kosovo area, sometimes allied with Bulgarian, Croatian, Hungarian, and Comintern terrorists. In spite of such activity, an increasing number of Kosovo Albanians began to realize that accommodation, if not assimilation, was the proper way to follow.

In the main, Serbian political parties took Kosovo seriously, seeing in it an opportunity to fill a vacuum and thereby collect some votes before others did so. The leading Radical Party, the strong Democratic Party, the broadly based agricultural bloc, and the Communist Party—all showed up in Kosovo. Already in 1919, the Kosovo Albanians formed their own political organization, called "Dzemijet." They held their annual congresses, published the group's paper *Moudjaeda* (Struggle), and conducted a variety of cultural programs. In the November 1920 elections, Dzemijet elected eight national representatives; in March 1923 this number grew to 18. Later the membership split, as many found that the strong and influential Serbian parties were of greater benefit and more likely to deliver. By the end of 1925, Dzemijet went out of existence, the former members either joined the pro-government coalition groups or the opposition coalition.

Joining a Serbian party did not, however, mean conversion, as later developments would show. In 1941, many of those who had joined Serbian parties became protagonists of Great Albania (under Italian occupation). They were the ones that Italian foreign minister, Count Ciano, had as early as 1939 called "daggers pointed in Yugoslavia's back."

If the political consciousness of the Albanian voter in Kosovo was not on the same level as that of most other Yugoslav citizens, it was not the fault of the Belgrade regime. Some of the accusations against Belgrade, even by well-meaning Western liberals, that Yugoslavia was running

a "political bastille" make no sense at all, and reveals a
pitiful lack of familiarity with the actual state of affairs.
Poorly or not at all educated Moslem voters (whether
Albanian or Bosnian) were easy prey to all sorts of political operators, susceptible to bribes, response to demago-
guery, and liable to be affected by various scare tactics.
In the Constituent Assembly elections of 1920, twenty-
two political parties and groups participated. Is this a way
to run a prison?! The Communist Party, which campaigned
as a champion of the "rights of national minorities to
independence, including the right to secession," came out
with 59 seats (out of 419). Many dispossessed Moslem beys
and hodjas cast their votes for the Communists (a protest
vote), and asked their followers to do the same.

What really mattered was that the Albanian minority in
Yugoslavia, thanks to its myopic leadership, made two
faux pas at the very beginning: rebellious, it chose the
wrong ally; introvert, it locked itself in its own cocoon.
The third, and indeed fatal mistake which it would make
much later was to accept the offer to develop within the
confines of that very same cocoon (the autonomous province).

Even when in the 1930s it became obvious that Albanians had finally begun to participate in Yugoslav day-to-
day reality—culturally, professionally, politically—the
residue of the unfortunate 1918 beginning was still noticeable. Perhaps there were too many people around who
would not let it be forgotten. Twenty years of the first
Yugoslavia were too short a span of time to let the process
of forgetting take place. When World War II came, the
bedlam started all over again. Now, after a forty year
lapse, forgetting seemingly is not even considered.

It may be instructive at this point to indicate what was
happening on the Albanian side of the border. In 1918,
as the war ended and the dawn of a new day came to
Kosovo, some 3,000 Albanian men, members of the "vol-
unteer army," were poised on the Albanian side of the

frontier, waiting for an order to go in and to liberate Kosovo. Their leaders were members of the Kosovo elite
that coordinated earlier "revolts" against the Turks at the
beginning of the 20th century. Many of them held high
positions in the Turkish bureaucracy, and some were members of the parliament in Constantinople (Hasan Prishtina,
Isa Boletini, Bajram Curri, Dervish Mitrovitsa). All of them
relentlessly bombarded the League of Nations with denun-
ciations of Belgrade. None of them paid any attention to
the political personalities that were emerging in Albania
itself: Ymer Vrioni, Evangjeli Pandeli, Bishop Fan Noli,
"flagbearer" Ahmet Zogu. The members of the Kosovo
Committee were over-confident, enjoyed full Italian support, and felt that they could even challenge the Tirana
government. Bajram Curri, a member of the Committee,
even assembled a few thousand warriors in the region of
Kukes, and sent them to fight the government.

In the years immediately following the world conflict,
Albania was still experiencing birth pangs, and had no
need for an arrogant committee from Kosovo. The country
was in strife; the liberals (headed by Harvard-educated
Orthodox theologian, Fan Noli) and the conservatives (led
by Ahmet Zogu) were seeking to control the government.
The Chieftain of the Mati tribe, Zogu, was either unusually
lucky or especially capable, because he rose to the position of the country's minister of interior at the age of 26.
In that position, he was ideally placed to watch the conspiracy work of the Kosovo exiles. He charged them with
obstructing the normalization of relations with a neighboring country, took away their parliamentary immunity, and
made it clear that he intended to bring Albania into the
family of Balkan nations. In the meantime, he became
head of the government, just in time to face the attempt
of the Kosovo exiles to overthrow him. That was either a
poorly organized coup attempt or Zogu's position was in
1923 far sounder and stronger than that of the Turkish
government in 1911. Kosovo bands in Albania were

crushed by Zogu's forces, with the support of some Yugo-slav units.

The internal situation in Albania, however, was far from stable. In February 1924, an assassination attempt was made on Zogu (in Vienna). In June, the liberals staged a coup, and Bishop Fan Noli formed the government, but his rule was short-lived. Looking for a foreign protector, he picked Moscow. That move alarmed the West, as well as King Alexander of Yugoslavia. Already in December 1924, Ahmet Zogu, leading a motley crew of Albanians, White Russians, and Yugoslav border troops, was back in Tirana, reinstalled as the future leader of Albania (1925-1939). After 1928, as King Zog I, he ruled by a combination of despotism and benevolence. He forbade Albanians to carry guns, outlawed archaic customs (such as vendetta), con-cluded several treaties with Italy and Balkan countries, secured internal stability, established the authority of the Albanian central government, and gave Albania a sense of national identity. Stavro Skendi describes Zog's contribu-tion as follows: "Whatever his flaws, he made a nation and a government where there had been a people and anarchy." (Cited in Paul Lendvai, *Eagles in Cobwebs*, Garden City, N.Y., 1969, p. 181.)

Relations with Yugoslavia were mixed. Zog conceded St. Naum (Ohrid) in exchange for another border point, but misunderstandings and distrust between the two countries continued. In 1926 Zog signed two pacts with Italy that gave Rome freedom of action in Albania. The Italian army built roads, fortifications, and airports that would later be used in attacks against Greece and Yugoslavia. In 1927, Albania broke diplomatic relations with Yugoslavia, but dialogue was reestablished shortly thereafter. Full mutual confidence, however, was never achieved. In the meantime, Albania had some contacts with Bulgarian ir-redentists and Croatian separatists, with Italian blessings. In 1937, however, Yugoslavia and Italy signed an agree-ment "not to permit, nor support, on their respective territories any activity that could harm mutual relations," which may explain why certain Bulgars and Croats had to be moved from Italy to Albania.

On January 21, 1939, Count Ciano and Yugoslav premier Milan Stojadinovich conferred in Belgrade about the "Albanian question." Stojadinovich was told of Italy's intention to occupy Albania, and apparently was promised Skadar in return, as well as the cessation of anti-Yugoslav propaganda with regard to Kosovo. A few days earlier, King Zog had recieved an Italian plan—in effect an ultimatum—for a reorganization of the state, which amounted to a loss of independence and practical annexation. With 30,000 Italian troops landing at four Albanian ports, Zog fled, and the Albanian parliament offered the Albanian crown to Victor Emmanuel III. In the meantime, Stojadinovich had resigned, and Ciano felt no obligation to his successor.

The Italian occupation was humilating to many Albanians, but the Kosovo Albanians felt rather good about it. Finally, the dream of a Great Albania was to become a reality, after the fall of Yugoslavia in 1941, even if under the aegis of the Italian crown. It meant a reverse of the Serbianization process in Kosovo, with encouragement by the Italians. It also meant the resurgence of hostilities, and the coming of civil war, both in Albania proper and in Kosovo. It meant a new beginning of an old, old struggle.

# CHAPTER XI

## MARXIST CONCEPTS OF NATIONALITY:
## THE COMINTERN AND THE BALKANS

Traditional Marxism holds that the capitalist system is the source of conflict between and among nationalities. Consequently, once a communist system was established, national animosities and hatreds would disappear. Peace and harmony would reign. Over the past several decades, however, this philosophical formulation has been the source of trouble and bitter controversy, especially among Balkan communists and their mentor, Josef Stalin.

In the Balkans, discussion of nationality problems from the Marxist point of view took place even before Stalin was born. One of the first, if not the first, to do so was a young Serbian student, Svetozar Markovich (1846-1875). Studying in St. Petersburg on a Serbian government stipend, young Markovich read Chernishevsky, Herzen, and other Russian writers, and subsequently moved in a circle of Russian socialists and anarchists (among them Bakunin) in Zurich. He became a socialist and used his considerable gifts in writing a number of political tracts. Fragile in health, he died at the age of twenty-seven, not long after his return from abroad.

With respect to the nationality question in the Balkans, Markovich believed that he had found the "master key" in the formation of a Balkan federation of South Slavs, where the peoples could live together on the basis of equality and self-government. He was interested in the liberation of South Slavs living under foreign rule. To that end he wanted to see the destruction of the Ottoman and Austro-Hungarian empires. He believed that his native Serbia could help in the liberation of brother Slavs, but he wanted to be sure that Serbia retained the image of "liberator" and not become an "oppressor."

Other Serbian socialists, notably Dimitrije Tutsovich (1881-1914) and Radovan Dragovich (1878-1906), founders in 1903 of the Serbian Social Democratic Party, followed essentially in Svetozar Markovich's footsteps. Tutsovich was critical of Serbia's desire to get an outlet to the Adriatic across Albanian territory, although if done by mutual agreement, he said, there could be benefits both to Serbia and Albania. He and his fellow Social Democrats believed, however, that Albania should be an "autonomous member of a democratic Balkan federation." Parenthetically, it should be noted that Tutsovich, unlike many other socialists, fought in the Serbian army against Austria-Hungary, and met his death on the battlefield in 1914.

South Slav communists, among them Sima Markovich and Josip Broz Tito, claimed to be heirs of Svetozar Markovich, and at different times espoused the idea of a Balkan federation. But they were never able to reach agreement on the operational aspects of such a federation. And some of them could not even approach a theoretical consensus.

The Yugoslav communists went through some bitter controversies over the nationality question. Their mentor, Stalin, as commissar of nationalities under Lenin, produced a brief book entitled *Marxism and the National Question*. Although full of confusions and evasions, the book's essential message is that national hostilities are the result of the conflicts of capitalist classes. If applied to Yugoslav-Albanian relations, for example, the Serbs and Albanians were at each other's throats because of their respective "bourgeoisies" were in conflict. By accepting such a formulation, Yugoslav communists theorized themselves out of their Balkan reality. Unless totally blind, they should have known that Serbo-Albanian disputes were not based on class struggle.

In 1923, a resolution of the Yugoslav Communist Party (then known as the Independent Workers' Party of Yugoslavia), stated that it is the duty of the Party to lead (with the organizations of the working masses of oppressed nationalities) a common and open struggle for the right of secession, i.e., to support the movements of oppressed nationalities with the aim of forming independent states such as Croatia, Slovenia, Macedonia, Montenegro, as well as the liberation of Albania.

This resolution and other discussions among Yugoslav communists led to considerable disagreement as to the national question and how it should influence the organization of a future communist state. Sima Markovich (no relation to Svetozar) became head of the Yugoslav Communist Party in 1926, and subsequently perished in Stalin's purges because Stalin, Dmitrov, Tito, and others did not agree with his views on the nationality question. Born in the heart of Serbia, and a brilliant mathematician, Markovich was a man ill-suited to blind obedience. In a brief pamphlet, he argued that there was not a nationality problem in Yugoslavia, but a constitutional one.

Markovich, along with other Serbian communists, were regarded by many other Yugoslav communists as "rightists." They were, in fact, accused of advocating Serbia's preponderance, the heavy-handed centralist concept of Belgrade's financial moguls (*charshija*). To avoid this image, they became the most vocal critics of nationalism, especially Serbian nationalism. Markovich did everything possible to project himself as a "leftist," progressive, and loyal to the international concept. He denounced the "imperialist tendencies" of the Serbian bourgeoisie, and asserted that the "Serbian theory of national unity of Serbs, Croats, and Slovenes is only a mask for Serbian imperialism." This was Markovich the "left wing" communist. Then in small print we read: "Of course we are talking only of state centralism. Because for the class conscious proletariat it is beyond question that for both the party and the trade unions centralism *must* be developed along the principles of proletarian democratic centralism." (*Nacionalno pitanje u svetlosti marksizma* [The National Question in the Light of Marxism]; Belgrade, 1923, p. 119.) The accusation that Sima was a "rightist" and a "unitarist" because he believed in central direction of affairs under communism, could subsequently be levelled at all top Yugoslav communists, including Tito himself.

Even before he became General Secretary of the Yugoslav Communist Party, Markovich had some close calls with the Comintern, the Soviet arm for world revolution. He could not easily accept the Comintern's support for the Revolutionary Macedonian Organization (IMRO), nor its objective of detaching Vardar Macedonia from Yugoslavia (in fact Serbia). Moreover, he argued that Macedonian, Bulgarian, or any other Balkan nationalism was just as "bourgeois" as Serbian nationalism. He could not see the Comintern's fine distinction between the nationalism of oppressed and oppressor nations. And he resented the thundering utterance of Comrade Zinoveiv (head of the Comintern's Executive Committee): "Macedonian Bulgarians, [Macedonian Bulgarians!], Albanians, Montenegrins, Croats, and Bosnians are rising up against the rule of the Serbian bureaucratic landowning oligarchy. . . ." Zinoveiv obviously knew little about Serbia, the society of free small landholding peasants. In general, it could be said that no Balkan state had yet reached Marx's two requirements for revolution: a mature capitalism in decline, and an urban proletariat.

The Comintern, however, had its way. At its fifth congress in Moscow in June-July 1924, admittedly a "congress of struggle for the Bolshevization of Communist parties," the resolution on Yugoslavia included the following passage: "The opinion of the Yugoslav delegate (Milojkovich) that the Yugoslav Communist Party must fight equally hard against any nationalism whatever, is not only opportunist, but objectively plays into the hands of the Great Serbia bourgeois nationalistic policy. In their struggle communists must always bear in mind the difference between oppressing and oppressed nationalities." And the July 1935 plenum of the Yugoslav Communist Party's Central Committee, meeting in Split, insisted that the Party "continue with full force our struggle against the regime of Great Serbian oppression, and for the liberation of oppressed peoples. . . . "

The same tone is found later in Tito's article, "The National Question in the Light of the People's Liberation Movement" (*Proleter,* December 1942), where he says: "Macedonians, Arnauts [Albanians], Croats, and others ask themselves in fear, 'what will become of us if things return to the old way'. . . . The question of Macedonia, the question of Kosovo and Metohija, the question of Montenegro, the question of Croatia, the question of Slovenia, the question of Bosnia and Hercegovina will be decided easily and to the satisfaction of all only when the people alone will decide. . . . "

No mention of Serbs or Serbia, but to the Albanians, ninety percent of whom (by subsequent admission of Yugoslav Communists) were at that time on the side of the Italian occupier, he found it expedient to pledge that they would be free to decide their future! Why were not the Serbs mentioned? Did all of the mentioned groups fear the Serbs? Who was it that would not permit them "alone" to decide? These questions alarm Serbs—communist and non-communist. The non-communists resent the tone of the suspicion about Serbian motives; the communists frantically attempt to prove that this is not what the questions imply.

When the time came for the Albanians to experiment with Marxism, the simplicity of the "master key" solution was not simple enough. It had one serious and rather complicating drawback. The center of communism was in Moscow. The Albanians were accustomed to turning abroad for guidance (Constantinople, Rome, Vienna), but to have Slavs direct their destiny was inconceivable. After all, the whole idea of the Albanian "national awakening" was kindled to save the nation from "Slav usurpers." Even if the incompatible was somehow accepted, many Albanians felt that competing with Serbs and Bulgars for Russian favor was a hopeless and suicidal task. There is reason to believe that communism, had it come from French or German socialists, would have been more palatable to Albanian intellectuals.

Nevertheless, as if part of some established historical pattern, once again what was supposed to be an indigenous Albanian movement, started abroad. It was imported as a package: organization, cadres, training, and dependence. As some kind of fatal damnation of all movements called Albanian, Marxism was just as foreign as Islam and Catholicism had been originally. To make matters worse, in the pecking order of the communist parties in the Third (Moscow) International, Albania was placed last.

The leading party body of the Albanian Communist Party was set up in Moscow in 1928. The Comintern arranged for the first party operatives to be sent into the country only a year later. This attempt did not produce anything meaningful; communism had no chance to participate in the political life of the new nation. King Zog's regime provided no room for communist agitation, and most of the Westernized intellectuals and liberals were not oriented toward the East.

For Serbo-Albanian relations, it was of some significance that the most prominent among the Albanian communists sent from Moscow was Ali Kelmendi. He was born in Pech. In 1930 he visited his hometown and Kosovo generally, worked closely with the Kosovo Committee, attempted some ground work in the area, but on the whole was not successful. In Albania itself, the Communist Party infiltrated the intellectual "kruzooks," where Marxism was tolerated in the guise of so-called "discussion groups," and among the followers of the former Fan Noli party (mainly in the southern part of the country). Ali Kelmendi and his few collaborators were forced to leave Albania in 1936. He took part in the Spanish Civil War and in 1939 died in France.

Soon after the Albanian Communist Party was formed abroad in 1928, the Yugoslav Communist Party held its fourth congress in Dresden, Germany. The resolution issued at the end of the deliberations included a paragraph dealing with Kosovo: "The Party declares the solidarity of revolutionary workers and peasants of the remaining Yugoslav nations, and first of all Serbia, with the Albanian national revolutionary movement, represented by the Kosovo Committee, and calls upon the working class to wholeheartedly assist the struggle of the dismembered and oppressed Albanian people for an independent and united Albania." (Quoted in Slijepchevich, *Srpsko-arbanaski odnosi,* p. 312.) This was when the Kosovo Committee was operating out of Vienna, under the aegis of the Comintern, which supported and coordinated some of the Balkan irredenta movements. (Nicholas C. Pano, *The People's Republic of Albania,* Baltimore, 1968, p. 27.)

There is little doubt that in the interval between the two world wars, the Communist Party of Yugoslavia was tragically wrong on the nationality question. For reasons of expediency and the benefit of a few wavering votes, the Party appealed to all those who felt "exploited" by the Serbs. The Croatian Ustashi, the Bulgarian irredentists, the disposed Moslem landowners, the Albanians and others— all joined the Communists in chasing the same nationalist "vampire," Serbia which allegedly was determined to dominate the other nationalities. Unfortunately for all of the Yugoslav nationalities, the result under Tito's Communist regime was a "national solution" which has bred divisiveness that has gone a long way toward tearing the fabric of Yugoslav unity, which the regime had avowed to achieve. As subsequent pages of this study will show, the "chickens have come home to roost," and the folly of a misguided nationality policy may pose a threat beyond the Yugoslav borders.

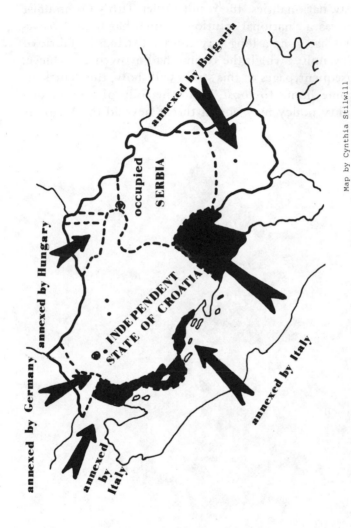

annexed by Bulgaria

occupied
SERBIA

annexed by Hungary

INDEPENDENT
STATE OF CROATIA

annexed by Germany

annexed
by
Italy

annexed by Italy

Map by Cynthia Stilwill

Partitioning of Yugoslavia in 1941

# CHAPTER XII

## KOSOVO, 1941-1945

On March 27, 1941, Yugoslav army officers (Serbs) overthrew the government that had signed the Tri-Partite Pact. In early April German and Italian forces attacked Yugoslavia, and following the quick collapse of military resistance, dismembered the country. Italy, which had taken over Albania in 1939 occupied large parts of the Adriatic littoral, and assisted Albanians in taking over Kosovo and adjoining regions. An Axis satellite, the so-called Independent State of Croatia, was set up under the Italian-sponsored Ustashi movement. Two Balkan members of the Tri-Partite Pact (Hungary and Bulgaria) were given parcels of Yugoslav territory. What was left of Serbia came under outright German occupation, ruled with an iron fist by the military commander. After twenty years of its existence, the state for whose creation the Serbs had made unbelieveable sacrifices was torn asunder.

Ironically, occupied Serbia overnight became a haven for Serbs from other areas. They were being killed or in other ways persecuted by the Ustashi in Croatia, the Moslems in Bosnia, the Hungarians in Vojvodina, the Bulgarians in Macedonia, and the Albanians in Kosovo. This incredible suffering of the Serbs in World War II has been the subject of a number of studies (for example: Edmond Paris, *Genocide in Satellite Croatia, 1941-1945;* Lazo M. Kostich, *Holocaust in the "Independent State of Croatia";* Herve Lauriere, *Assassins au Nom de Dieu*).

In Kosovo, the Albanians felt that their dream had been realized. Kosovo was annexed to rump Albania and became a part of "Great Albania," ironically by courtesy of the man (Mussolini) who in 1939 had destroyed Albanian independence. As a result of the collapse of the Yugoslav army, Albanians in Kosovo availed themselves of caches of arms, were recruited into local militia units, automatically became Italian citizens, declared themselves in support of the quisling Albanian government in Tirana, and began settling personal accounts with the Serbs in the area.

The Albanian quisling premier, Mustafa Kruje, visited Kosovo in June 1942 and publicly advocated the need of making Kosovo and Metohija a pure ethnic entity. The most efficient way of doing it, in his opinion, was by removing the Slavs from the area: old Serbian settlers moved out; newcomers liquidated. Postwar Yugoslav studies of this policy (e.g., S. Miloshevich, *Izbeglice i preseljenici na teritoriji okupirane Jugoslavije, 1941-45* [Refugees and evacuees on the territory of occupied Yugoslavia]; Belgrade, 1981, pp. 53-55) indicate that between 70,000 and 100,000 Serbs were forced to leave the Kosovo area. According to a one-time member of the Central Committee of the Comunist Party of Serbia, Tito did not permit their return after the war.

Kruje's proposal was an expression of Albanian euphoric satisfaction with the fulfillment of their national aspiration. That it was achieved through the humiliating Italian occupation was of lesser significance.

The rounding up of Kosovo Serbs produced two major concentration camps, in Prishtina and in Kosovska Mitrovitsa. They served as labor reservoirs for the Trepcha mines, control over which the Nazis had retained, and for the fortification works in Italian-held Albania. Many of them also ended up as slave workers in German-occupied Europe. There were some who were transferred to camps in Serbia proper, and thereby felt relieved. Unfortunately, many of them perished in Nazi reprisal executions for acts of sabotage by Yugoslav resistance groups.

As a general rule, most vulnerable in occupied Kosovo were Serbian "colonists," i.e. those who had come to Kosovo within the past three decades, but those settlers who farmed in far away villages were also an endangered species. With Albanians on a rampage, Serbs had two choices: flee or fight. Those who decided on resistance found former Royal Yugoslav officers, just emerging as a resistance organization, their most logical choice. The Chetniks of Colonel Draza Mihailovich were, in fact, the first underground resistance group in all of Europe. Members of the communist movement were at that time still lying low, theorizing about the "war of bourgeois imperialists," which they thought the Soviet Union would sit out.

The assimilation process, especially of Serbian children, was in full swing from the very beginning of the occupation of Kosovo. Instruction in the schools was carried out only in the Albanian language. There were, however, few Serbian children in elementary schools. Parents were afraid to send them, and the authorities did not insist. In principle, high schools were not open to Serbian youngsters.

Serbs were considered Albanian citizens only in *de jure* matters, by virtue of their domicile, but not in other respects. The Bishop of the Ras-Prizren diocese, Seraphim, was interned in Albania, and later died there. The abbot of the Devich monastery, near Kosovska Mitrovitsa, lost his life in resisting two raids on church property. Yugoslav historians have never attempted to estimate the material damage, the loss of life, and human suffering generally, of the Serbs in Kosovo during World War II, because it was one of the thematic taboos in postwar Yugoslav historiography. Now when it might be possible, there are no records.

In 1941, Albanians in Kosovo had no representative
mass organizations of their own. The Communist Party of
neighboring Albania was nonexistent. It was to be formed
only some six months later. Having only a few cadres of
their own in Kosovo, Albanian Communists were always
part of the Montenegrin Communist organization. The
regional committee of the Communist Party of Yugoslavia for Kosovo and Metohija was formed in 1937, but
only as an extension branch of the Montenegrin committee. Insignificant as a unit, Albanians were never asked
to send delegates to All-Yugoslav Communist assemblies.
Even as late as November 1943 (Second Anti-Fascist Council of National Liberation of Yugoslavia), there was not a
single Albanian among the 146 attending delegates. The
histories of Yugoslav Partisan movements in Yugoslav
territories during the war years, which document in great
detail various "spontaneous mass uprisings against the occupier," never mention Albanians. If they do, it is peri-
pherally in the context of Macedonian or Montenegrin
resistance.

In 1940-1941, according to available Yugoslav Communist archival sources and memoir literature, all Yugoslav Communist Party attempts to reach Kosovo Albanians
were either unresponsive or unrewarding, and in some
cases downright frustrating. Top Communist organizers,
such as Vlado Strugar and Svetozar Vukmanovich-Tempo,
were still working on it as late as November 1943, when a
regional committee of some sort was finally formed. In
fact, there were in all of Kosovo and Metohija only three
communist leaders from the old days who were available.
Vukmanovich points out that "conditions for [starting]
armed resistance in Kosovo and Metohija were worse than
in any other region of the country. . . . the Albanian population, which made up two-thirds of the whole population,
had an unfriendly attitude toward the partisans. . . . The
occupiers have succeeded in winning the Kosovo Albanians to their side by annexing Metohija and a part of

Kosovo to rump Albania; the local government is in the hands of the Albanians, the Albanian language is obligatory. . . . The Albanian population is suspicious of all those who struggle for Yugoslavia, whether old or new; in their eyes it is always less than what they have got from the occupier. . . . " (*Revolucija koja teče* [Revolution in Development], Belgrade, 1971, p. 338.) Vukmanovich also asserts that he came to the conclusion that the "formation of partisan units in that region" was premature. Consequently, he decided to form Kosovo units in areas bordering on Kosovo, mainly from Serbs and Montenegrins who had either left earlier or were at that time coming over to the communists. With no base among the local Albanian population, and with the Serbs mostly sympathetic to the Chetniks, Vukmanovich had no choice but to keep a distance for a while.

There was another important consideration that slowed down communist organizing efforts. That was the question of leadership, should it be Montenegrin (Serbian) or Albanian? This proved to be a great stumbling block. The Montenegrin communists obviously did not know how to handle it. They wanted it for themselves, but the Albanian masses would not follow a Montenegrin leader. If, on the other hand, the Albanians were to lead, the Serbs would balk. Later it was decided at a higher level that for the time being (i.e., until the end of the war), the Albanian partisans would fight under the Serbian communists. The solution was awkward, illogical, and an ever present threat to future relations.

Vukmanovich describes the mood of the population, predominantly Albanian, as "radically changed," following the annexation of these regions to Albania. "Power is in the hands of the Albanians . . . and this is all they see today." He depicts the city of Debar at the moment of its supposed liberation: ". . . all over the place Albanian flags. No Yugoslav or Macedonian flag at all. One would think that he is somewhere in Albania, not Yugoslavia. . . .

The units of Balli Combetar [Albanian nationalist group] control the city, and they are intent on using force in order to keep Debar as part of Albania. Albanian partisans, on the other hand, are no match for them, and in addition, they are not willing to oppose such intentions of Balli Combetar anyway." (Ibid., p. 370.) Vukmanovich admits that Yugoslav Communists could not force Albanians in their ranks to fight Albanian quisling troops. He even had to face an open insurrection of Yugoslav partisan units made up of Kosovo Albanians, which "resented being stationed in Macedonia" (ibid., p. 382).

There were some additional ominous signs as well. Even when the Montenegrins finally managed to form partisan units manned by local Albanians, these units were named after notorious protagonists of Great Albania. For example, the "Bajram Curri" unit was named after a prominent member of the famous nationalist emigre Kosovo Committee in Albania, and a one time minister of interior.

The wartime situation in Kosovo was reminiscent of Turkish times, in the sense that Albanians were returned to positions of power and the anti-Slav (i.e., anti-Christian) mood prevailed once again. The irony of it was that, while the privileged status of Moslems in Turkish times was to be expected, it now seemed weird by virtue of the fact that it was being pushed by Italy and Germany. Once Italy capitulated in 1943, Germany continued to follow the policy of making Albanians the privileged nationality.

The most dreaded organization in the area (under German control) was the "Kosovo Regiment," the cloak and dagger shock troops of racist Albanianism. It had the political blessing of the so-called "Second Prizren League," the wartime assembly that hailed and legalized the activities of the "Regiment." When Italy capitulated, the bulk of the Italian army supplies went to the "Kosovo Regiment." In collusion with Balli Combetar elements, some Moslem priests, and Albanian chauvinists, the Regiment

made sure that none of the acquired privileged positions
would be lost or weakened in the last turbulent years of
the war, 1944-1945.

Communists were the first (and only) among the resistance groups to realize that promising some of the acquired
advantages in a future Yugoslavia was the only way to win
the Albanians over to their side. Moreover, the Yugoslav
Communists were advocates of a new Yugoslavia, while
the Chetniks were looked upon as a return to the old ways.
In addition, the former promised a federal arrangement in
the new multinational state. This had a great appeal to Albanians, even to non-communists. The latter were convinc-
ed that there would be some room for Albanian nationalists. Besides, as the war was coming to an end, many of
them concluded that of the two evils, communism looked
incomparably better. Communist promises certainly
seemed attractive.

The Resolution of the First Conference of the People's
Liberation Committee for Kosovo and Metohija, held on
December 31, 1943-January 2, 1944, reads in its most
pertinent part as follows:

> The Kosovo and Metohija area is a region predominantly popu-
> lated by the Schipetar people, which has always as today,
> desired to unite with the land of Schipanija. Consequently,
> we feel obliged to point to the right way the Schipetar people
> should follow in order to reach its goal. The only road for
> Schipetars of Kosovo and Metohija to unite with Schipanija
> is to join in the common struggle with the other peoples of
> Yugoslavia against the occupiers and their servants. Because
> this is the only way to win liberty, when all peoples, includ-
> ing the Schipetars, will be in a position to declare themselves
> regarding their fate, with the right of self-determination, in-
> cluding the right to secession. Guaranteeing this is NOVJ [Na-
> tional Liberation Army of Yugoslavia] as well as closely
> associated NOVS [National Liberation Army of Schipanija].
> In addition, this is guaranteed by our great allies, the Soviet
> Union, Great Britain, and America.

The document from which the above was taken was published by the People's Committee of the Autonomous Province of Kosovo-Metohija, in Prishtina in 1955. The promise of self-determination, including the right of secession, would return to haunt the Yugoslav Communist regime.

One should not overlook the fact that the First Conference of the People's Liberation Movement of Kosovo and Metohija was not held on Yugoslav territory, but in the village of Bujan, in Malesia (Albania). Of the 51 delegates attending the meeting, only seven were Serbs or Montenegrins, while ten of the delegates were Albanian citizens who never lived in Kosovo or Metohija. An analysis of the names of the nine members of the Presidium shows positively that only one seems Serbian.

It should be noted that the nationalist wing of the resistance (Chetniks) could never have issued or signed such a politically flexible document, promising concessions that were not meant to be carried out. To the former Yugoslav officers such an act would have been regarded as treason.

Not so, says a man who signed the document, and at that time secretary of the Regional Committee, Pavle Jovichevich. Forty years later, in an interview with a Yugoslav periodical (*NIN*, December 11, 1983), he said that it was the only possible political move under the prevailing circumstances. Since Kosovo-Metohija had no "liberated" territory at that time, he says, the meeting was held in Albania. Moreover, Kosovo-Metohija was the only region where "partisans armed forces did not disarm a single Italian solider at the time of capitulation." There were a number of questions not yet clarified, such as the Party's "recognition of the annexation of Kosovo-Metohija to Great Albania," and the idea of "celebrating Albanian flag day," which "was perceived as anti-Serbian and anti-Montenegrin in essence." Another sensitive issue was the "proposal not to mention the name of Yugoslavia in any official pronouncements of the Party."

As a document of political expediency, needed to serve an opportunistic purpose, the Resolution presumably did not mean what it means today. In 1943, the Yugoslav Communist Party could afford to be generous in its promises, when the question of the future boundary between Yugoslavia and Albania seemed irrelevant. Albania itself was to be incorporated into Yugoslavia as a separate federal unit. Communists in the Kosovo-Metohija area were subsequently instructed not to enter into boundary discussions under any circumstances, but only to point out that "it will be solved in brotherly harmony and co-operation" (ibid.).

Moreover, says Jovichevich in his *NIN* interview, the boundary question between Yugoslavia and Albania was finally taken off the agenda once and forever in July 1945 in Prizren, at the time when the Regional People's Committee of Kosovo-Metohija "decided to make Kosovo and Metohija part of the People's Republic of Serbia." As it has turned out, however, the boundary question may not be a burning issue, but the treatment of Serbs and their monuments in Kosovo is certain to continue as a vital issue for Yugoslavia in the 1980s.

It is of interest that the Communist Party of Albania (founded and sponsored by Yugoslav Communists) did not address itself to the Kosovo problem either in its first declaration or later, which many Kosovo Albanians interpreted as a "sellout." Albania's Communists today maintain that this was the result of a common view, i.e., that "the question of the future of Kosovo and other Albanian regions in Yugoslavia should not be raised during the war. . . that Kosovo Albanians should fight fascism within the framework of Yugoslavia. . . that the problem will be resolved after the war by the two sister parties. . . and the Albanian people itself" (Enver Hoxha, *With Stalin*, 1981, pp. 137-138).

Hoxha's statement is corroborated by Tito's letter of October 9, 1943, to Miladin Popovich, the actual founder of the Albanian Communist Party (killed in Prishtina after the war by an Albanian youth): "Do not let various Albanian reactionary elements manipulate and attract Albanian masses by playing up the question of annexation of regions such as Metohija and Kosovo to Albania. . . . The question of freedom, national equality, and self-determination will be justly decided only through a common struggle with the People's Liberation Movement of Yugoslavia" (*Politika*, November 23, 1983). In a letter to Popovich, forwarding Tito's instructions, Ivan Milutinovich (a top Montenegrin Communist) adds: ". . . do not ever allow yourself to take the position . . . which would have this part [Kosovo-Metohija] annexed to Albania . . . it first has to be liberated in a common struggle . . . ." We know that Tito and his comrades were locked in a mortal struggle with Mihailovich's Chetniks, and therefore needed any and all able-bodied fighters to help tip the balance in their favor.

Mihailovich's guerrilla organization also had Kosovo very much in mind. Not only was Mihailovich's struggle a part of a general concern for national preservation, but being a professional soldier, he could never forget the strategic military value of the region. A key point in a possible Allied advance through the Balkans—which scared the hell out of Balkan communists—Kosovo was seen by Mihailovich as a communication line that would be extremely vulnerable unless held by the Serbs (and not Bulgars or Albanians). By early 1942, therefore, he had three firmly established task forces in the area, covering Metohija, Kosovo, and the Ibar river basin. In time four more brigades were formed and incorporated into two Kosovo Corps. He held a secret air strip in the area, which was used for night landings of transport planes from Cairo. The Movement deteriorated later, in the face of the steady strengthening of Albanian forces, and Tito's determination to seize power.

Vukmanovich-Tempo was apprehensive until the last moment that British and US troops might invade the Balkans.

He warned the Macedonian and Albanian communists never to trust the Allies, who would "bring back the old government," and would "demand the disarmament of forces that fought against the occupier . . . . We will never let Allied forces to even step on our land. Only the forces which have won the victory over the occupiers can organize the elections for the new government . . . . " (*Revolucija koja teče*, p. 359.) This was music to Albanian ears, because they certainly could not have wished—after all they had done in the war—to see the Allies come and make decisions about their future.

Vukmanovich's apprehensions, however, were misplaced. The Allies abandoned Mihailovich and the nationalists, who, after waiting for four years to "save Kosovo," found themselves manipulated into a corner without an exit. In the end, they could only helplessly watch Yugoslav partisans and the army, aided by two Albanian divisions, enter Kosovo. The two Albanian units came at the explicit request (September 1, 1944) of the Communist Party of Yugoslavia, sent to its sister party in Albania, to participate in common operations in Kosovo and Macedonia.

In the great chase after the retreating German forces that ensued, Serbia found itself temporarily invaded by 20 Soviet, 10 Bulgarian, and two Albanian divisions—a total of 32 foreign divisions—sent by governments, which in 1941 were either neutral or allied with Germany, at the time when the Serbs decided to say "no" to Berlin!

# CHAPTER XIII

## THE CPA-CPY CONNECTION, 1941-1948

When Hitler attacked the Soviet Union in June 1941, communists everywhere were eager to help the motherland of communism. But how? The Yugoslav Communists had an underground organization, but not the Albanians. In Albania there were groups of frustrated intellectuals, mostly western educated, who wanted to serve their country. A few were communists, but most of them were Marxist-oriented liberals who were unhappy with the political, economic, and cultural level of the Albanian masses. The few communists wanted to pool the scattered energies of all disgruntled individuals and groups into an organized movement. The immediate problem was that there were no Albanian communist cadres or party organization to carry out policies and instructions. From one point of view, this was a good thing, because it offered an opportunity for a fresh beginning, with no burdens from the past.

A clandestine meeting was called in Tirana on November 8, 1941, where members of all these scattered groups were introduced to two experienced Yugoslav Communist organizers, Miladin Popovich and Dushan Mugosha, sent to

148

help the Albanians organize the Albanian Communist Party, which in turn would organize a leftist resistance movement. Enver Hoxha, son of a Tosk Moslem land-owner from Gjirokaster and a one-time government stipendist in France and Belgium, was elected Secretary General of the new Albanian Communist Party. The puppet government of quisling Kruje was thus faced by a puppet resistance leader, Hoxha. Since that time until the Stalin-Tito break in 1948, the Communist Party of Albanian (hereafter referred to as CPA) remained an appendage of the Communist Party of Yugoslavia (here-after referred to as CPY).

More recently, Albanian Communists, with Enver Hoxha in the forefront, have been trying to project an image of resentment because of that appendage arrange-ment. However, the resentment must have been the best kept secret in Albania, because the newly-founded party was a carbon copy of the CPY in every respect, inside and out. On September 16, 1942, the National Libera-tion Front was founded (in Peze)—dominated by clan-destine communist cadres—with the task of coordinating guerrilla warfare against the occupier. In July 1943, an important conference of the Central Committee of the CPA was held in the village of Kucake (near Korce), at-tended by Yugoslav instructors. In those "two years of happy and promising start"—as Enver Hoxha himself characterizes the CPY-CPA connection—Kosovo and its fate were simply ignored in public pronouncements. In his book, *The Titoites,* published in Tirana in 1982, Hoxha says: "The Party issued many statements about its stand on the national question, but in none of them did it make a clear pronouncement on the future of Kosovo and the other Albanian regions after the war. This could not fail to disturb and confuse the Albanian population of these zones. . . . " (p. 87).

In the spring and summer of 1943, however, "in meet-ings and quarrels with [Tito's emissary] Vukmanovich-

Tempo," according to Hoxha, the question exploded full
blast. Tempo complained about Albanian Communists
who display "Greater Albania sentiments" and the tendency to become "a reserve of the enemy." The disgruntled Hoxha allegedly replied: "It has never been the custom of the Albanian people to unite with the enemy . . .
that they have their mind on Albania, this is no more than
natural. And don't attempt to change their minds, because
you will never succeed. For them the national question is
vital and this is precisely the point that should be grasped.
. . . In my opinion it is quite out of place for you to employ the expression of 'greater Albania'." (p. 89)

Now it was Tempo's turn to be "gravely offended," and
he demanded an explanation. He got it, Hoxha's way:

> Comrade Tempo, the slogans and concepts of 'greater Albania'
> or 'lesser Albania' have been anti-Albanian slogans and con-
> trary to the objective historical truth. . . . We have never
> raised the question of 'greater Albania' or 'lesser Albania' and
> never will . . . reactionaries of every kind . . . through these
> anti-historical and anti-Albanian fabrications . . . want to
> alienate our people from the Party and sabotage the National
> Liberation War. . . . In short, Comrade Tempo . . . we use the
> term 'greater Albania' only on these occasions and in this
> sense, and will never permit it to be thought that since we at-
> tack the bearers of the pseudo-slogan 'greater Albania' we are
> allegedly in favor of some 'lesser Albania'. . . . We are for the
> Albania which, both as a territory and as a nation, is one and
> one alone. (Ibid., p. 90.)

Hoxha is probably right when he now tries to convey
the impression that in 1942-1943, many Albanian Communists could not follow the Yugoslav logic of having the
Kosovo Albanian partisan units under the command of
the CPY. If Kosovo was part of Albania, as they believed,
if Albanians were one indivisible people, with their own
Communist Party, why should some Albanian fighters be
commanded by Albanians and others by Yugoslavs? Moreover, Albanians were suspicious of the idea of one over-all

"Balkan Staff" leadership, which would coordinate the policies and actions of all Balkan communist parties. The Albanian staff, says Hoxha, "would be under the command of . . . the 'Balkan Staff,' which undoubtedly would have to be led by the new 'strategist' of national liberation wars, Josip Broz Tito" (p. 92). Eventually, the whole idea was discarded.

The Albanians' creeping suspicions were in part attributable to Vukmanovich-Tempo, whose overbearing attitudes did not always suit his position as "Tito's ambassador." He was known for his inclination to behave like a "bear in the green house" (Tito's description). But there was more. Another CPY Central Committee member (Ivan Milutinovich) apparently echoed similar attitudes somewhat later when two Albanian delegates brought to Montenegro some requests for urgent aid. On their return, the two reported in dismay to Hoxha: "There is another Tempo in Montenegro [Milutinovich] . . . . He accused us of being 'Great Albanians'." (Ibid., p. 103). Then came Tito's letter of December 6, 1943 to the CPA. Hoxha states that in that letter Tito accused the leadership of the CPA of maintaining "the stand which the reactionary Albanian bourgeoisie maintains" (ibid., p. 104). Hoxha believes that Tito's lecture came as a result of Albanian constant prodding as to "why the CPY considers it right to demand the 'immediate' unification with Yugoslavia of a zone inhabited by Slavs [Istria] and did not consider right the analogue case of Kosovo and other regions torn from Albania" (p. 106). There they were, two sister communist parties, who thought that they had found the magic recipe for the solution of the national question, futily exorcizing themselves of bourgeois nationalistic vampires!

A turning point in the CPY-CPA connection seems to have been the moment when in 1943 the Yugoslavs demanded that the Albanian Communists disassociate themselves from their entanglement with the nationalistic movement, Balli Combetar. At the meetings in Labinot, and Kucake, Vukmanovich had warned his Albanian comrades that Balli Combetar had adopted the "same tactics as the Chetniks in Yugoslavia," i.e., to avoid confrontation with the occupier and to wait for the Allies to disembark. It was not a good idea, therefore, to plan on setting up a joint National Liberation Council that included Balli Combetar. Nevertheless, in July and August 1943, representatives of the two movements met in the village of Mukaj, and reached an agreement on collaboration. Balli Combetar at first insisted on a demand that Kosovo remain a part of Albania after the war, but finally agreed to let the question be decided after the defeat of the Axis. The CPY, however, wanted to eliminate the Albanian nationalist movement. At a stormy session of the top CPA body, Hoxha, realizing that he was in a minority, exercized self-criticism, and soon thereafter the Albanian partisans attacked the Balli Combetar. From September 1943 (when Italy capitulated) until November 1944 (when the CPA installed itself in Tirana) full scale civil war raged in Albania.

Following the Yugoslav example, the National Liberation Front created the Albanian Anti-Fascist Liberation Council, which in turn proclaimed itself the national government, forbade King Zog to return, and consolidated its grip over the liberated territories. It is of interest to note that of all East European "socialist states" emerging after the war, Albania was the only one that was spared the presence of Soviet troops. The installing of Albanian Communist rule in Albania was the product of a well-oiled coordination of strange partners: the CPY provided the political guidance, while the Anglo-American command in Italy made it possible for Albanian Communist units to be amply supplied. The whole ascent of Enver Hoxha seems unreal: two partners who disliked each other supporting the bastard who hated the guts of both of them!

The Albanian question was never raised at either Teheran or Yalta. Albania was a non-person country, plainly and truly a "quantite negligeable." Of course, Stalin was very much aware of Albania's position as a satellite of Yugoslavia, and to visiting CPY leaders in January 1948, he said: "We have no special interest in Albania. . . . You ought to swallow Albania—the sooner the better." (Milovan Djilas, *Conversations with Stalin*, New York, 1962, p. 143).

As the war ended, Belgrade was the first to recognize the government in Tirana, and in July 1946, the two governments concluded a Friendship and Mutual Assistance Pact. War-ravaged Yugoslavia provided Albania with extensive economic, military, and cultural aid, as well as schooling and professional training for Albanians in Yugoslavia. Bilateral treaties were signed, a customs union was set up, and monetary conversion agreements concluded. Be it noted, Yugoslavia got very little in return. Yugoslavia also sponsored proposals for Albania's admission to the United Nations and other international agencies.

In October 1947, Hoxha expressed his appreciation for the many Yugoslav favors, stating: "Our state is moving ahead and will progress because it has at its border Marshal Tito, who is supporting us to develop our country, to improve the life of our people. Yugoslavia, together with the Soviet Union, is protecting us from the American imperialists." (Vladimir Dedijer, *Jugoslovensko-arbanski odnosi, 1939-1948* [Yugoslav-Albanian Relations]; Belgrade, 1948, p. 97).

Disagreements arose, however, after the Yugoslavs sent a squadron of military aircraft to Albania, in response to an alleged but phoney danger of possible intervention from Greece. The Yugoslavs insisted on a military pact and a unified command, which meant putting the Albanian army under the command of a Yugoslav general. Hoxha was in a state of panic, yet it seemed that there was little that the Albanians could do. In desperation, Hoxha pulled out his ace card—he appealed to Stalin.

Hoxha was still in the coachman's seat, but the reins of power were not solely in his hands. Several Albanian leaders were obsessed with the Yugoslav magic, acting as Yugoslav stooges and impatiently waiting for the signal to execute a putsch. Hoxha pretended that he did not know why the Yugoslavs were in such a hurry for an amalgamation with their satellite. It is difficult to believe that he did not know about Stalin's increasing dissatisfaction with Tito. By that time, Hoxha had visited both Moscow and Sofia, two cities that were always eager to pick up a good story about Belgrade. In July 1947 Hoxha did complain to Stalin about "some Yugoslav aircraft which had landed in Tirana, contrary to recognized and accepted rules of relations among states," which prompted Stalin to ask: "Are your people not happy with the relations with the Yugoslavs?" (Enver Hoxha, *With Stalin,* Tirana, 1981, p. 73).

Earlier events did not bode well for the future. In midsummer 1946, Tito hosted Hoxha in Belgrade and at Lake Bled, in two former royal residences. Three aspects of the visit struck the visitor: (1) the "scandalous luxury" of his host's life style, (2) the itinerary excluded Kosovo, (3) the host's failure to appear at the farewell dinner at the Albanian Embassy. Among topics discussed by the two leaders were the Kosovo problem, allegedly brought up by Tito, who wanted to know how Hoxha felt about the subject. "I went on to express to Tito the opinion of the Albanian side that Kosovo and the other regions in Yugoslavia inhabited by Albanians belonged to Albania and should be returned to it. The Albanians fought in order to have a free and sovereign Albania with which the Albanian regions in Yugoslavia should now be united. The time has come for this national problem to be solved justly by our parties" (Hoxha, *The Titoites,* pp. 284-285). According to Hoxha, Tito replied: "I am in agreement with your view, but for the time being we cannot do this, because the Serbs would not understand us." In his earlier reference to this conversation, Hoxha quotes Tito as having said: ". . . Serbs would not understand such a thing" (*With Stalin*, p. 140).

Another sensitive subject that was touched upon in these conversations was the question of Balkan federation, which Hoxha maintains was never explained clearly to him by the Yugoslavs. Moreover, when Tito and Bulgaria's Dimitrov discussed federation, Hoxha was piqued because he was not informed about the talks, just as the Macedonian Communists were not.

When Stalin got wind of these talks, as well as of Yugoslavia's pressures for a Yugoslav-Albanian military merger, he made it known to the Yugoslavs that such major moves in the socialist camp were inadmissable without the blessings of Moscow.

When in June 1948, the Cominform split with Tito became public, it took Hoxha only 24 hours to denounce his yesterday's benefactor as a "traitor" and a "Trotskyike." Moreover, he says that he told Soviet leader Andrei Vyshinsky that the Belgrade leadership had followed a "chauvinistic policy" toward Kosovo "both during and after the war" (*The Titoites,* p. 533).

In researching the crux of the CPY-CPA relations, a major problem is in coping with Hoxha's amazing aptitude to reverse himself. He apparently thinks nothing of stating in his more recent writings some things that fly in the face of what he wrote earlier. Yugoslavs, of course, do not hesitate to reprint his original statements, but the Albanians in Albania have no way of reading them. For instance, Hoxha now states that Tito's "advice" and "instructions" of December 1942, "arrived too late to effect the issues and, consequently, were no longer of any value." (Ibid., p. 31.) Hoxha chooses to ignore his own writing in the publication, *Albania-Yugoslavia,* published immediately after the war: "The Yugoslav Partisan experience represents a priceless treasure to us, of enormous usefulness in our struggle. Tito's letter marks a historic event in the history of our people." (*Enver Hodzina Albanija* [Enver Hoxha's Albania]; Belgrade, 1981, p. 31).

Moreover, Hoxha now says that the two Yugoslav emissaries (Miladin Popovich and Dushan Mugosha) had "no special role" whatever in founding and directing the functioning of the Albanian Party (*The Titoites,* p. 37). The Yugoslavs have, however, produced Hoxha's letter which he sent to Tito when Popovich was returning to Yugoslavia in 1944, in which he says: "We would show ample lack of gratitude if we failed to mention the great indebtedness our party feels toward two Yugoslav comrades—Miladin and Dushan. . . ." (*Enver Hodzina Albanija,* p. 35.) What seems to bother Belgrade most is that Tirana's increase in ingratitude paralled Yugoslav pampering. In Tito's own words: ". . . at the times when we were carrying out agreements [Treaty of Mutual Aid, Friendship and Cooperation] which basically were detrimental to Yugoslavia." (Ibid., p. 262.)

Thus ended the seven-year long rosy chapter of sisterly party love, and Marxist experimentation in solving the national question—in profound repugnance and intense hatred.

Yugoslavia

Map by Cynthia Stilwill

# CHAPTER XIV

## KOSOVO IN THE NEW YUGOSLAVIA

Tito, in seeking to win over the Albanians of Kosovo during his wartime struggle to seize power, led them to believe that after the war they would have the right of self-determination, including the right of secession, as we pointed out in chapter twelve. But his decision at the end of the war to make Kosovo-Metohija an autonomous unit within Serbia was not warmly received. Nevertheless, several other actions of the Tito regime began to change the character of Kosovo-Metohija rather radically in favor of the Albanians. As indicated in chapter twelve, some 100,000 Serbs were forced out of Kosovo during World War II, and they were not permitted to return. Moreover, with each passing year, more and more Serbs were forced to leave, between 150,000 and 200,000 in the twenty-year period, 1961-1981. In the meanwhile, in the period after the war, between 200,000 and 240,000 Albanians were brought in from Albania to the Kosovo-Metohija region. And over the years, Kosovo Albanians gained increasing control over events in the province.

Nevertheless, at the very beginning of the new Yugoslav regime, there were considerable difficulties between the Albanian masses and their "liberators." For example, the Kosovo Albanians resisted the "voluntary mobilization" drive. In some cases they simply ignored the appeal, and had to be herded together in their mountain villages, marched down to check points, and transported under armed escort to recruiting posts. Animosity grew and became intense. In one instance a shoot-out developed, leaving 200 Albanians mowed down. In another, 130 Albanians suffocated when cramped into a former gunpowder depot. The founder of the Albanian Communist Party in 1941, Miladin Popovich, now back in Prishtina, was killed by a Balli Combetar member, who walked into his office and murdered him in cold blood. It was in that evolving atmosphere that the Supreme Command of the People's Liberation Army issued a decree on February 8, 1945, placing Kosovo under military administration. In a month's time, the backbone of the opposition was broken. Ironically, it was broken by those who had praised Dimitrije Tutsovich (pre-1914 Serbian socialist) for castigating Serbian bourgeois military methods in dealing with nationality issues!

In 1948, the Yugoslav minister of interior (Rankovich) reported to the party congress that past "weaknesses and mistakes" of the Communist Party were in large part responsible for the difficulties. He said that the Party was wrong when it took the position that Serbian partisan units could not survive in Kosovo during the war because of the "chauvinist attitudes of the Schipetar masses." Secondly, the party was wrong because it had "a sectarian attitude in bringing people into the fold of the anti-fascist front." Rankovich did not, however, mention the fact that during the war Kosovo Moslems looked to Albania as their natural ally, and that there were few if any communists in the area to associate with. Nor did he cite the fact that at least half of the Serbs in the region were

overtly or covertly pro-Chetnik. He did admit that the
problem of "re-educating" the Kosovo Albanians to soften
their opposition to Slav communists had proved to be a
rough one.

From the time of the incorporation of Kosovo-Metohija
into the People's Republic of Serbia as an autonomous
region, it became Serbia's responsibility to demonstrate
flexibility, and to adopt the right approach to the Kosovo
Albanians. Solid preparatory political education and economic support were the right combination, or so believed
Serbia's Communists. For a time it seemed as if the formula
would work. As the Republic of Serbia kept steadily in-
jecting aid (economic, cultural, social) into the region,
Albanian postwar resistance mellowed, extremists lost
their preponderance, and those advising forbearance and
self-control gained the upper hand. Some of them were
card-carrying communists, others were not, but both never
lost sight of the national Albanian cause in multi-national
Yugoslavia.

The Yugoslav central government, for its part, had made
a commitment to change the way of life in the backward
Kosovo-Metohija area. In spite of all difficulties that it
encountered, it did not want to see that commitment short-
changed. With all available intensity, it set out to reach its
aim—to win over the Kosovo Moslems, just as it had sought
to do in the case of the Bosnian Moslems. The former, as
reluctant as they may have been, finally obliged. They cud-
dled comfortably into the new concept, as they began to
realize the advantages.

For the Serbian Communists the problem was somewhat
compounded by the fact that they had to break through
two barriers simultaneously: anti-Serbian and anti-Marxist.
In politically educating the Kosovo Albanian masses, the
Kosovo Communists in fact had the task of re-directing the
political thinking of the two-thirds majority of the population, from thinking Balli Combetar to thinking Socialist
Alliance. The best way to succeed, they thought, would be

to give the Kosovo Albanians what they always craved for: regional autonomy in managing their affairs, cultural identity, the right of self-determination, even the right of secession (declaratively). In the postwar federalistic euphoria there was nothing that the Yugoslav central authorities could have done in terms of pointing to the disintegrating pitfalls of the experiment, lest they be blackened and calumnated as "reactionaries."

What began as the "Autonomous Kosovo-Metohija Region" (1947), became the "Autonomous Province of Kosovo and Metohija" (1963), and ended up as the "Socialist Autonomous Province of Kosovo" (1969). These may seem as insignificant semantics, but under Yugoslav conditions it meant ascending from a faceless geographic entity to a "constituent element of the federation." The 1969 formula was subsequently used by the Albanians to demand the status of a republic in the Yugoslav Federation, which could in turn lead to the riddance of Serbia's tutelage. This scary possibility dawned upon the Serbian Communists only later, when the statistics on the rapidly growing Albanian majority became alarming.

Economically, Kosovo was moving ahead in unheard of leaps, with an annual industrial growth rate of 30 percent. With eight percent of the Yugoslav population, Kosovo was allocated up to 30 percent of the Federal Development Funds. The Kosovo authorities, it was discovered later, used large sums from these funds to buy up land from Serbs and give it to Albanians, clearly a misappropriation. Investment loans were given for periods as long as fifteen years, with a three year grace period, and an interest rate of a mere three percent.

Kosovo, always considered one of the "underdeveloped" areas of Yugoslavia, now received priority treatment. In a five year period in the 1970s, for instance, some 150 million dollars were pumped into it annually. Moreover, of one billion dollars of World Bank development credit to Yugoslavia, Kosovo got 240 million or 24 percent. It is

estimated that within the past decade, some 2,100 million
dollars have been poured into the Kosovo economy. Much
of the cultural support, social services, and educational aid
was never to be repaid (i.e., financed by Serbia or the
federation).

In view of all this aid, it is often asked, how come Kosovo persistently lagged so far behind other parts of the
federation? Why is it among the poorest regions of Yugoslavia? Demographic reasons are usually cited, the Kosovo
area having a birth rate of 32 per 1,000 (the highest in
Europe), and the largest families (6.9 members). If all of
Yugoslavia had grown at that rate its population today
would be 50 million instead of 22 million. Other explana-
tions given are Albanian backwardness, lack of management skills, corruption, investing in unproductive prestige
enterprises, unrealistic and over-ambitious planning, and
growing unemployment (27.5 percent).

Still others point to paradoxical overeducation in the
region. The perennial Kosovo illiteracy problem has been
on the way to obliteration: within the first few years after
the war, 453 elementary schools, 30 high schools, and
three institutions of higher learning were opened. Prishtina,
a city of about 170,000 has over 50,000 college students
and 40,000 high school students. For every 1,000 inhabitants of Kosovo there are 30 young people working toward
a college degree which will get most of them nowhere,
partly because only 20 percent studied science and tech-
nology. Kosovo has some 450,000 high school and university students who compete for 178,000 working places
in the whole regional economy, and about 46,000 of those
are in the nonproductive sector. A Yugoslav sociologist
has pointed to the tensions and pressures that such "un-
controlled explosion of education" created among the
Kosovo elite, who in their unsatisfied urge to succeed became "easy prey" to nationalistic views.

The Albanians tend to blame others for their plight; they
are prone to accuse the other republics and nationalities

of "exploitation" and see themselves as victims. Can it be
that aggressive Albanian nationalism, which used to accuse
Serbs of not educating Kosovo Albanians, will now charge
Serbs with over-educating Albanians? The real answer to
the question of the under-development of Kosovo is not
in its lack of progress but in the comparative rates of development, which in other areas is four to six times higher.
Distancing themselves from other Yugoslav peoples by in-
sisting on a separate, ethnically pure, narrow Albanian cultural orientation (which makes them unemployable in a
lingusitically Serbo-Croatian work environment), Kosovo
Albanians have isolated themselves from the rest of the
Yugoslav community.

While the economic lag is felt by both Albanian and
Serbian inhabitants of Kosovo, the cultural isolation is a
singularly Albanian phenomenon. This is why Kosovo
Serbs resent being forced to learn Albanian and to attend
schools with instruction in the Albanian language. It is
paradoxical indeed that Serbian efforts to bring Albanians
in, only contributed to keeping them out; that the federa-
tive philosophy of freeing peoples for the sake of individual
development and the broadening of inter-nationality ties,
in fact imprisoned them in their own nationalistic confines. Serbian Communists are asking themselves in disbelief: after all we have done for Kosovo, is it possible
that the Albanians are less happy in the "new communist
Yugoslavia" than they were in "rotten royalist Yugoslavia?"

The question is asked because of the unrest, demonstrations, and protests that have taken place in the region
in 1968, during the 1970s, and especially in 1981. And
because the communists themselves admit that "the
atmosphere is fraught with something bad." Ali Shukrija,
one-time Chairman of the Presidency of the Socialist
Autonomous Province of Kosovo, put it this way: ". . . one
enters a shop and the salesman behaves strangely. One
enters a butcher's place, the transitor hums, Tirana is on.
One switches on the TV set in Prishtina, and does not

know if he is in Tirana or here. . . . And then the enthu-
siasm for folklore: incredibly aggressive. . .one can see
Tirana all the time, the lights directed that way. . . . "
(Interview printed in *Borba,* May 10-12, 1982).

Shukrija should not complain. It was the Kosovo Communist leadership that turned the heads of Kosovo Albanians toward Tirana. They did it in their nationalistic
ecstasy, when they got rid of the allegedly Serbian-domin-
ated state security service in the late 1960s. At the time
that Shukrija heard the radio in the butcher shop hum-
ming, the Kosovo security service was in the hands of the
Albanians. They were probably listening to the same tune.
Shukrija does not tell. It seems perverted logic, therefore,
to blame Serbs for the 1968 demonstrations that occurred
in several Kosovo cities.

Following the 1968 disorders, in which a number of
persons were injured, most of the Albanian demands were
met. One was not: republic status for Kosovo, but they
soon got it, in fact if not in name. The 1968, 1971, and
1974 amendments to the Yugoslav constitution, one after
another, granted Serbia's autonomous provinces the pre-
rogatives of republics. Kosovo got its own supreme court
and its own Albanian flag. Belgrade University extension
departments at Prishtina were upgraded to the level of an
independent university. This is when the leaders of Prishtina's youth turned away from Belgrade and toward Tirana.
Belgrade could not provide either Albanian teachers or
Albanian textbooks.

Tirana was more than glad to oblige. In ten years (1971-
1981) it sent to Kosovo 240 university teachers, together
with textbooks written in the Albanian literary language.
At the same time came the aggressive folklore that Shukrija
was talking about: Albanian historic and socialist movies,
Albanian TV and radio hookups, sport and cultural exchange visits. The amalgamation was in full swing. In plain
view of the Kosovo Albanian leaders. The latter did not
wake up even in 1974, when an alleged "Cominform group"

was discovered, or in 1976, when a "movement for the national liberation of Albania" surfaced. When Serbs complained of pressures and "reverse discrimination," their voices seemingly could not be heard because of the ever more vocal clamor of the Kosovo Albanians.

Finally, on March 11, 1981, a routine evening in the student cafeteria turned into turmoil when a wild bunch of youths began demolishing everything that they could get their hands on, which was subsequently depicted as a student protest at the "lousy" food they were getting. After they had beaten up the cashier, broken chairs and window panes, the demonstrators took to the streets of Prishtina, where they were faced by the riot police. Several policemen were injured as well as students, who were dispersed. The demonstrators reappeared on March 26th, this time in the early morning. Allegedly, they blocked the entrance to three student dormitories in Prishtina, and talked the students into attending a mass meeting where "student privileges" would be discussed. This was when political slogans were displayed that had nothing to do with student problems.

In their enthusiasm, the young ring leaders decided on a show of force in another section of the city, by attempting to disturb the running of the so-called "Tito's relay," the annual youth event celebrating the President's birthday. It proved a mistake. The police reacted, and in the ensuing fracas 23 protestors and 14 militiamen were injured. Then on April 1st, as demonstrations spread to other Kosovo cities, with political demands dominating the riots, three groups of demonstrating citizens assembled in front of the building housing the Kosovo Province Committee of the Communist Party in Prishtina. According to a Belgrade weekly (*NIN*, April 12, 1981), the slogans read: "Kosovo-Republic," "We are Albanians, not Yugoslavs," "We want a unified Albania" . . . By the time the evening was over, two demonstrators and two militiamen had been killed.

A member of the Presidency of the Central Committee of the Yugoslav Communist League [Party], Stane Dolants, held a news conference in Belgrade on April 6th. Alleging that the Party leaders had been caught off guard by the riots, he depicted the Kosovo events as the consequence of the "horrendous dynamism of the progress of our society, dynamism which in 36 years spanned in essence one whole century. . . . " He said that the melee was the deed of "two to three hundred hooligans," that the "Kosovo militia was 80 to 90 percent Albanian" and that the two militiamen that were killed were both of Albanian nationality. When it was all over, the Yugoslav press reported that eleven persons were dead and 57 wounded.

Tirana sources, as well as some Albanian sources in Yugoslavia, insisted that one thousand or more persons were killed. One American Embassy source in Belgrade estimated that 200 to 300 were killed. It would seem certain that the number killed was far greater than the Yugoslav press reported.

At the above-mentioned press conference, Dolants tried to minimize the significance of the continuous migration of Serbs from Kosovo, but at the Devich monastery near Prishtina, Mother Superior Paraskeva seemed to be running a better data collection center than the Central Committee of the Party in Belgrade. Standing in the monastery courtyard, and pointing her finger to the surrounding mountains, she spilled out data with the precision of a computer. The delivery was somewhat monotonous, if distressful: "Let us start with the village of Poljana, 48 or 49 [Serbian] families, all gone; Kraljitsa, 68 families, all gone; Ljubovats and Dugovats, around sixty homes, all gone; Gornje and Donje Prikaze, 30 homes, all gone; Klina, some 28 families all gone; Novo Selo, 28 families, all gone; Lavusha, there were 25 homes, all gone; all these people moved out; Oluzha, there were twelve homes, all gone; Trstenik, some 45 families, all gone; then Chikatovo, at one time 60 homes, and Glogovats with 70, no one around any more;

Brochana, 28 families, all gone; Krsh Brdo, 18 families, all gone; Ludovich, of 12 families not a single one there. Then this village over there, Banja, well this one I don't know."

The stunned reporter interrupts the litany: "But where did all these people go?" "To Serbia, where else," responds Mother Superior, matter of factly. She then related how she and her sister nuns, 30 of them, lived since 1947. In a state of actual siege, battling the Albanian youths who harass them day and night, throwing stones, raiding the monastery forest, vegetable gardens, animal sheds. ". . . I was beaten, had broken ribs, my head was bloodied ten times. . . . We must say the militia came often, but what's the use. . . ." But how do you defend yourself, asks the reporter. Mother Paraskeva looks at him for a moment, then adds: "God protects us, who else?" (Mother Paraskeva's interview was published in the Serbian Orthodox Church publication, *Pravoslavlje,* May 15, 1982).

How come a Serbian nun was so well informed? There are two reasons: first, her personal interest in the people she knew so well, and second, the Holy Synod of the Serbian Orthodox Church in May 1969 instructed all ecclesiastical personnel of the Ras-Prizren diocese to collect all pertinent data on all instances of attacks on the clergy, churches and church property committed by citizens of Albanian nationality in the Kosovo area. This order resulted from growing expressions of concern and alarm, both from members of the Serbian population of Kosovo and from Serbian priests who thought that the leadership of the Serbian Orthodox Church in Belgrade was not doing much to protect the Serbian faithful. Even after the Kosovo riots of 1981, such expressions were heard. For example, in February 1982, an "open letter" was addressed to the Holy Synod of Bishops by a group of priests from the deanery of Tamnava (town of Ub in Serbia proper), asking the Serbian Episcopate "why the Serbian Church is silent" and why it did "not write about the destruction, arson, and sacrilege of the holy shrines of Kosovo."

The Holy Synod of Bishops had appealed to the official authorities of the Republic of Serbia, as well as to the Federal Executive Council, listing concrete cases, but the situation was not rectified. So on May 19, 1969, the bishops appealed to President Tito. In his reply of May 23, he expressed his regrets, and agreed that the reported incidents were in violation of the constitution. He promised to do everything possible to prevent such incidents and lawless acts, and "to secure for all citizens a safe life as well as the security of their property." He wrote that their letter, together with his stated opinion on the need of taking firm steps for the protection of the law, would be sent to the Executive Council of the Assembly of the Socialist Republic of Serbia.

This exchange did not, however, mark a change in the safety of Serbian sacred places in Kosovo, nor did it alleviate the deep-seated worries of Serbs in the area. The migration of Serbs and Montenegrins from Kosovo continued, and was becoming one of the most pressing political issues for the Serbs generally who knew about the situation. Naturally, it was the Serbs who were most deeply and emotionally concerned, both with the issue of migration and the continuous trend of Albanian vandalism against Serbian monasteries, churches, attacks on the Orthodox clergy and nuns, desecration of cemeteries and national monuments.

Life had become increasingly unpleasant for the Serbs and Montenegrins, not so much because they were a minority, but because of the pressures to leave Kosovo. Direct or subtle, these pressures involved discriminatory practices at work, obligatory instruction in Albanian in the schools, lack of influence in politics, threats of various types, the stealing of livestock, and the futility of appealing against seizures of personal property to courts staffed by Albanians. Thus, faced with general animosity and outright pillaging, the frustrated victim finally decides to abandon everything and flee.

Indicative of the trend are the population statistics. In 1946 the Albanians made up about 50 percent of the population of Kosovo, but by 1981 it was 77.5 percent. The corresponding percentage for Serbs and Montenegrins had dropped to about 15 percent (Yugoslav statistics list Serbs and Montenegrins separately). Thus, as the Albanian goal of an ethnically pure Kosovo became a reality, that reality became increasingly unbearable for those who could not pack up and leave.

According to the findings of the Kosovo Special Committee that inquired into the matter of emigration, in the period 1971-1981, over 57,000 Serbs and Montenegrins moved out of the area, confirming the continuous nature of the trend. Parents found that their children had been intercepted while going to school or coming home. Serbian women were raped. Serbian girls were assaulted or kidnapped by Albanians. Farmers found their crops damaged. Elderly citizens who stayed home got letters or telephone calls that upset their peace of mind. Unfriendly slogans or symbols were sprayed on the walls of Serbian homes under cover of darkness.

The Kosovo Albanian authorities were also anxious to break up the compactness of Serbian areas. To do this they would, for example, build a factory in a solidly Serbian settlement. Under the population key of the Yugoslav government, 80 percent of the workers in that factory had to be Albanians, who then would be brought in, and thus break up the compactness of the Serbian settlement.

Two years after the 1981 events, Belgrade's *Politika* (June 3, 1983), headlined in big letters: MONTHLY—400 EMIGRANTS. The article reported that 10,000 Serbs and Montenegrins had moved out of Kosovo in the previous two years. Kosovo as a whole, it reported, has 1,435 settlements, 666 of which are without a single Serb or Montenegrin, and in 147 settlements they make up only three percent of the population.

Another reporter (for *Pravoslavlje*, May 15, 1982) tells of two Montenegrins seen digging in the cemetery of the village of Petrovats: "We moved out in the early spring, but come back to get our deceased mother. . . . It became unbearable here any longer. Now that the village is called Ljugbunar, we could not have a water system, but the Albanians are getting it. There is electricity now, and a paved road as well, but what's the use, there was no place for us here any more. . . . "

The chronology of complaints against Albanian aggressiveness as published in the periodical of the Serbian Orthodox Church (*Glasnik,* July 1982) reads in part:

1969:  the ruins of the ancient Serbian church near Veliki Trnovats were converted into a rest room, and a donkey was found inside. . .

1970:  the cellar of the Dechani Monastery was broken into several times. . .

1971:  the Orthodox cemetery in Petrich, all tombstones smashed and the accacia forest trees cut. Albanian youngsters attacked Serbian women on their way to the service in St. Nicholas church in the village of Mushutishte, near Prizren. . .

1972:  the main door of the church in the village of Vinarats, near Kosovska Mitrovitsa, was found broken and removed; the same damage was done to the church in the village of Dobrchan, near Gnjilane; in Prizren the church of St. Nicholas was repeatedly damaged; in the village of Shipolje, near Kosovska Mitrovitsa, fifteen tombstones were smashed; in the village of Srbovtsi, eight tombstones, and in the villages of Opterusha, Orahovats, and Ratinje, the same thing. The monastery woods in Mushutishte raided twice this year, some 30 trees cut down. The nuns who opposed the vandals were beaten and exposed to the worst obscenities. Forest trees belonging to St. Demetrius monastery in Preshevo were cut down and sold openly at the local market. . .

1973:  an Albanian cutting a tree on church property
       wounded the priest who tried to stop him; St.
       Mark's monastery church was found with the
       main door removed, the iconostasis smashed,
       books torn, and candleholders bent [the same
       church was later vandalized every time it was
       repaired] . . .

1977:  Ras-Prizren Bishop Pavle assaulted by an Alban-
       ian youngster, who grabbed his beard, shouting,
       "Hi preacher," and hit him over the head. The
       incident occurred in the center of downtown
       Prizren . . .

1979:  eleven young Albanians raided the Gorioch mon-
       astery, shouting insults at the abbot; an unsuc-
       cessful burglar set fire in the stable of the Soko-
       litsa monastery; Devich monastery nuns were
       assaulted several times and the property plun-
       dered . . .

1980:  a professor of the theological school in Prizren
       was injured in a street attack; the woods of the
       Holy Trinity monastery near Prizren, raided by
       five Albanians who cut 64 trees; in the night be-
       tween March 15/16, at 3 A.M., the old guest
       house building—with one wing serving as a lib-
       rary and the other as a reliquary—of the Pech
       Patriarcahte monastery was set afire and burned
       down . . .

1981:  ten windows of the Saint Urosh church in Uro-
       shevets were broken; thirty eight tombstones
       at the cemetery of the village of Bresja, and six
       in the village of Shtinga smashed; the church at
       Uroshevats raided once again, irredentist slogans
       written on the wall of an adjacent building . . .

1982:  cemetery tombstones in the yard of the church
       in Kosovska Mitrovitsa were broken; the Devich
       monastery lost thirty trees from its woods, the
       monastery sow was found killed with an axe,

and the access road blocked by bulldozed huge stones.

Does all of this look like ugly Albanian nationalism or just plain vandalism on a rampage? Serbs and Montenegrins are traumatized, especially since they are getting no answers. Kosovo leaders, such as Ali Shukrija, admit publicly that Kosovo events "have disrupted relations... traumatized Kosovo Albanians as well, I can state that openly. It has been a shock to them too...." (*Borba,* May 10-12, 1982).

But such declarations do not satisfy Serbs and Montenegrins. They are looking for deeds not words. They see no energetic and prompt intervention by local authorities, no attempt to bring to justice those responsible for such acts. They want stiff sentences, purging those in authority, and the clear-cut establishment of who is responsible for all of this: the entire Belgrade policy or the particular interpretation of that policy by the Kosovo leaders? After all, the President of the Kosovo Provincial Committee of the League of Communists is a member of the Presidium of the party's Central Committee. Does he not report to his comrades in Belgrade what is going on in Kosovo? Don't they ask him about what they must have read in the papers or were told by the Patriarch's office? Is this some kind of conspiracy of silence, a cover-up, a snow job? Questions, questions, questions.... With the degree of independence that the Yugoslav media have today, such a hot issue cannot just be swept under the rug.

True, there have been a few trials, closed to the public. Why closed? Members of "illegal" organizations have gone to prison. But what of Kosovo's top Albanian leaders? Two have resigned publicly. Is resignation the extent of their penalty? The rector of Prishtina University, the editor of the literary journal, and a few provincial government secretaries were removed from their positions, but slated for other jobs. Is this any way to deal with persons in leadership positions?

What really caused disaffection in Serbian and Montenegrin public opinion was that Kosovo security forces and
the police were unable to come up with the identity of the
arsonist or arsonists who set fire to the Pech Patriarchate
monastery. That blaze shook Serbian public opinion. But
the more that Belgrade insisted on learning the truth, the
less it got. Kosovo officialdom clammed up. The news-
hungry Serbian press began its own investigative reporting,
and that made everybody unhappy. The Kosovo Communists accused the reporters of being snoopy sensation seek-
ers, Croatian and some Serbian Communists felt that such
efforts were counterproductive, but the broad public did
not get what it really wanted: an official response and not
news reports.

At this stage, the issue is not only complex, but so emo-
tion-laden that it may be too much to expect clear thinking
A Belgrade University professor, an ethnic Albanian (Halit
Trnavci), denounced "the blind nationalistic fanaticism"
of the Kosovo Albanological Institute and the Kosovo
Academy of Sciences, and asserted: "By their declaration
of hatred and intolerance toward the Serbian and Montenegrin people in the Kosovo area, they harm the Kosovo
Albanians first of all. . . . We all know that Kosovo har-
bors the most important and greatest monuments of Serbian medieval culture. For centuries, throughout the rule of
those who were our common enemies. . . hundreds and
thousands of Albanians protected those Serbian monuments like their own homes, their own children, like their
own national shrine. . . . " But can such an appeal reach
the minds of his compatriots in Prishtina, drugged by nationalist euphoria?

And what about those Serbs who agree with the prominent author and one-time Tito protege, Dobritsa Chosich,
who stunned his colleagues at the Serbian Academy of
Sciences when he publicly asked: "What kind of people
are we Serbs, that so many of us laid down our lives for
liberty during the war, only to see that that victory deprived

us of freedom?" And what of Serbian Communists who
agree with Serbia's highly placed party and state leader,
Dragoslav Markovich, when he said: "After all, Serbia's
Communists cannot eternally be considered responsible
for the sins of the Great Serbian hegemonistic bourgeoisie!"
(*Politika,* December 26, 1981.)

Evidence seems to be accumulating that Serbia's pati-
ence may have reached its limit, and that the "red flag"
of "Serbian hegemonism" will not be accepted any longer.
Forebearance is one thing, but resignation, submission, and
acquiescence in their own defeat, especially on the Kosovo
issue, is historically un-Serbian. Unless Marxism has won
over nationalism and blunted the Serbian sense of history,
Serbs cannot become disinterested in their own heritage.
Judging by the surge of national intonation in numerous
literary works, theater pieces, movies, and art works, the
Serbian spirit is very much awake. It is very much alive
in intellectual circles, unabashedly evident in the ranks of
the youth, displaying national symbols and singing old
nationalistic songs, and manifested by the emergence of
popular respect for the role of the Serbian Church in the
latest national plight.

Today books about Serbia's history are best sellers.
Contemporary literati, writing about the sufferings, massacres, and sacrifices under the Croatian Ustashi, Bosnian
Moslems, and Albanians, suggest that the reaction of Serbs
may lead to dangerous disillusionment with the official
slogan of "brotherhood and unity." As Serbia gropes
trying to recharge its atrophied national spirit, those who
contributed to the atrophy seem concerned that they not
find themselves outside the mainstream of Serbian public
opinion. It is clear that 1984 is not 1944. One wonders
if to Serbian Marxists there is a crucial difference between
being out of touch with one social class and being out of
touch with the whole nation?

# CHAPTER XV

## THE FUTURE

What of the future? Aggravated conflict or dialogue and a solution? At this writing (early 1984), there seems to be an impasse, a stalemate. One is tempted to ask: are the recent actions of Kosovo Albanians a replay of past Kosovo scenarios, of weak central authorities unable to prevent Albanian pogrom tactics?

Three years after what the Yugoslavs call the "counter revolution" in Kosovo, and two years after the Central Committee of the Yugoslav Communist Party (officially League) adopted what is known as the "Platform on the Kosovo Problem," most Yugoslavs feel that not enough has been done to deal with Kosovo-Albanian nationalism. Neither side is satisfied—emigration of Serbs continues, the question of republic status for Kosovo is still dangling, theoreticians of "blood and soul" (unification with Albania) are still whispering. Some tactical accommodation is practiced by the top Yugoslav Communist leadership, allegedly to achieve a "rapprochement" with its Kosovo segment. Serbia's top Communist, Dragoslav Markovich, defined the situation in Kosovo in brief when he said: "There is no reason to underestimate what has been achieved so far, but even less reason for self-satisfaction, in view of how much still remains to be done . . . . " (*NIN*, December 25, 1983). Many Yugoslavs (Communist and non-Communist) tend to believe, however, that Markovich is "whistling in the dark." In their opinion, if there has been progress, it has been at a snail's pace at best. A large number of Serbian Communists are bitter toward the Kosovo Albanians for what they regard as gross ingratitude, but they refrain from manifesting that feeling publicly.

The federal authorities in Belgrade, aside from establishing a military presence and exercising a watchful eye, have not engaged in a direct interference in Kosovo affairs. Similarly, the Republic of Serbia government, although constitutionally empowered to intervene, has been disinclined to do so, believing that any direct action would be counterproductive. Hence, both federal and republic officials have sought only indirectly to influence the Kosovo Communists in the hope that they would work themselves out of the situation that they in large measure had helped to create.

And local Kosovo authorities are "unwilling or incapable of preventing lawlessness, even when concrete proof exists and complaints are made against particular individuals . . . . The incompetency of the authorities and unequal treatment of citizens of different nationalities cannot but create uneasiness among the Serbian population and encourage the nationalists in their crimes." (*Politika*, March 19, 1984).

At the other end of the spectrum are Serbs who believe that the Communist Party approach is only a pious hope that the problem will go away. They demand that Serbs who were displaced from their homes in the Kosovo-Metohija area be allowed to return, and that compensation for material damage to their homes, churches, and other establishments be made from American assistance to Yugoslavia. In addition, they demand that all Albanian inhabitants of Kosovo-Metohija, who are there as a result of post-World War II immigration, be returned to Albania. Moreover, they demand that the human rights provision of the Helsinki Accords be applied to the Serbs. Understandably, there are no public media channels in Yugoslavia through which these opinions and demands could be expressed.

Another body of Serbian opinion holds that Kosovo Albanians now have an opportunity to make a historic choice, which often comes only once in the lifetime of a people, to become a positive force for Yugoslav stability. They have a chance to change their image. To do that they would need to demonstrate their willingness and ability to achieve a rational reconciliation with Serbia. They would need to show to everyone concerned their firm desire to allow to others what they so vigorously demanded—and obtained—for themselves. The proof of their sincerity would be in the change in their attitudes toward the Serbs in Kosovo, toward Orthodoxy, toward the Christians and their holy places.

The answer to the question of whether the Kosovo Albanians will attempt to continue living in the past or seek to move to the future, seems uncertain. A large amount of ink is being poured out by Kosovo Albanian academicians (notably Ali Hadri and Skender Rizaj) denouncing "Serbian discriminatory practices" (both royalist and communist). Moreover, faced with Serbian historical rights, Kosovo Albanian intellectuals are over their heads in researching their past, trying to prove Illyrian or Thracian descendance. To the centuries of Serbian presence in Kosovo, they counterpose the Albanian national awakening (Prizren League, 1878). To the independent observer it seems ridiculous to attempt to equate three centuries of Serbian nationhood with a hastily organized Constantinople-sponsored three-day meeting late in the nineteenth century. Even more mindboggling, it would seem, is the contention of the Kosovo think tank (Albanological Institute) that there were no massive Serbian migrations in the

17th and 18th centuries due to Albanian and Turkish actions. Instead, the Serbs simply ran away in an effort to escape the Black Death plague!

The point in referring to these Kosovo Albanian statements is not to deride them, but to suggest that what has happened in the recent past cannot be a fruitful scenario for the future. Kosovo needs to come out of its present economic, ethnic, and psychological straight-jacket. But will Kosovo Albanians do it? Will they try? As of this writing (1984) the situation does not seem too hopeful. In all of the polemics coming out of Kosovo, one still has to see in print or hear a Kosovo official say something along this line: "Look, Hoxha, Kosovo is a part of Yugoslavia (Serbia), and we want to live in Yugoslavia as Albanians, but even more as Yugoslavs."

Today's Prishtina, a city of impressive hotels and administrative buildings, new residential sections, and broad boulevards, is enveloped in a depressive atmosphere. Its streets are teeming with a strikingly young population, and many Albanian children growing up in an ethnic prison. These students are open-eyed, future-oriented, and impatient, and not the children of the past as are their teachers. Will the Kosovo leaders, who have chained them to the 4,000 or so square miles of Kosovo, realize that these young people are interested in Yugoslavia and their future in it, and not in whether they hail from the Illyrians?

Kosovo Albanians cannot have their cake and eat it too. If Kosovo wants to retain its "dependent" status, expecting the rest of the country to aid it as the least developed region, it will have to forego the luxury of doing what it pleases with the money it gets. Moreover, there are limits to what the country can do for Kosovo. Yugoslavia is exhausted in pulling the cart of non-alignment, burdened by a 30 to 40 percent annual inflation rate, and a 22 billion dollar foreign debt. Kosovo may want to become a "little California," but neither Serbia nor Yugoslavia is a little America.

The opening gambit toward change was made by the Yugoslav Communist Party after World War II. It offered Serbia's sacred territory to be governed by the local ethnic majority. Among the numerous kibitzers of this political chess game were many who doubted the wisdom of the opening gambit. Kosovo Albanians satisifed themselves by taking the sacrificial pawn, but refused to yield anything in exchange. Kosovo Albanians may find themselves on a dangerous course. They may lose what they perceive as their advantage. They cannot wrest Kosovo out of Serbia's body by force; that much they should know. If they decide to use force, force they will get.

The Serbs are waiting. The present uneasy balance cannot last forever. Which will it be: sharper confrontation or reconciliation? Some form of assimilation in the Yugoslav context? All depends on who makes the next move for the Kosovo Albanians—the same old guard, or a new team looking for different horizons. It has to be the latter, if Serbia is to stay in the game. No game, no autonomous Kosovo.

Some ask, can Serbia and Montenegro abandon their nationals to the mercy of the Kosovo Albanians? And, is it possible that one day, Serbia and Montenegro may feel bound to join forces and invade Kosovo, as they did against the Turks in 1912? In this dreadful context, the question posed in 21 Serbian Orthodox priests and monks sounds ominous: "Who is it that dares to take upon himself the responsibility before history, that in his time Kosovo was lost ethnically and spiritually?" (*Pravoslavlje*, May 15, 1982.)

In this connection, it is interesting to recall the words of the lucid Serbian member of the United Opposition in pre-1941 Yugoslavia, Dragoljub Jovanovich, on the question of the Serbo-Albanian future. ". . . there is no Yugoslav government that would dare to deliver them [Schipetars] to Albania, even if they should unanimously declare themselves for such a move. There could be talk of resettlement but by no means could Kosovo and Metohija be turned over to any other state that is not Slav, and which could at any moment become booty of a non-Balkan power." (Jovanovich's personal notes in the author's possession.)

It must be recognized that the ethnic content of the Kosovo area has changed, but that does not make the Serbian holy places any less sacred. In the past, as long as the Kosovo Albanians did not disturb the Serbs and the sacred monuments (in some instances the Albanians actually guarded them), an atmosphere of "live and let live" prevailed, and the multinational structure of Kosovo was not pertinent.

In the Balkans, ethnic imbalances are a fact of everyday life, ethnic jealousies a way of life, ethnic jokes the salt of life, and ethnic conflicts a curse of life. But all of this is a part of Balkan living.

What of the demand for republic status for Kosovo? It was turned down decisively as early as 1969, but that does not mean that the question could not be reconsidered. If republic status were to be granted, however, a pandora's box would be opened that could lead to all sorts of destabilizing dangers to the territorial integrity of Yugoslavia. Constitutional revision would be needed, with everyone getting into the act. The autonomous province of Vojvodina would have to be given republic status. And Croatia could no longer continue to disregard the fact that over one-half million Serbs live within its borders. By viewing themselves as the mother country of all Albanians in Yugoslavia, the Kosovo Albanians have been charged with interfering in the internal affairs of other Yugoslav republics, notably Macedonia and Montenegro. Open resentment was expressed by the latter two at a session of the Central Committee of the Yugoslav Communist Party (*NIN*, December 25, 1983). The Macedonian delegate noted, with some bitterness, that in the last ten years 21,245 Albanians came to his republic, while only 5,000 departed.

Where does all of this leave the Yugoslav Marxists? While they may not wish to recognize it, instead of solving the sensitive nationality problem, they have made it worse. Kosovo has demonstrated to any one who wants to see that a coherent entity cannot be created by playing up particularisms and separate identities. Territorial and ethnic separatism, which was an effective weapon in the struggle for power, became a murderous scalpel when in power. The multinational credo of postwar Yugoslavia proved destructive, forcing the central government constantly to shore up what local nationalisms destroyed.

They may not wish to admit it, but the Yugoslav Marxists have come full circle on the nationality question. They are now where the Yugoslav monarchists were six decades ago, even though their phraseology may seek to hide it. Ironically, the "great truths" that today's Yugoslav Marxists are discovering were known to Yugoslav "bourgeois" politicians many years ago. One is tempted to ask: was it necessary to experiment for several decades to discover that one nation is not the sum total of many nations. The formula of 6 plus 2 = Yugoslavia, may look good in a puzzle on the entertainment page, but not in the cabinet of the prime minster. The healing effects for the Yugoslav Marxists may be painful, but perhaps it is better late than never. There may be some satisfaction in seeing ones compatriot sobering up even after many years, but one cannot avoid asking, why did he have to get intoxicated in the first place.

In a wider sense, it is interesting that the Kosovo events of the early 1980s have had a widespread impact in all parts of Yugoslavia and on its political, economic, military, and social spheres. For the time being, at least, there seems to be a strong, and potentially far-reaching, trend away from federalism and toward unitarism (depicted as "democratic centralism"). Everywhere there is a condemnation of exclusivity (*zatvorenost*), i.e., the earlier trend toward republic and province particularism, toward isolation from other parts of the federation. The new stress is on discipline, reliability, resourcefulness, and responsibility.

There is an increasing unwillingness to contribute to the country's central fund, without verification of expenses, the nature of the distribution of funds, the wisdom of investments—in a word, more control by centralized management. No more self-management unless it is responsible and produces results.

Whether the Yugoslav entity be political, economic, cultural, or social—whether the person involved be a party official, a military strategist, a technocrat, or enterprise executive—all seem to detest two favored Yugoslav slogans, "lako chemo" (easy does it) and "nema problema" (no problem). They hate the eight-centered (six republics and two autonomous provinces) impotence of the decision-making process, the eight-bureaucracy implementation of decisions, the eight-variant approach to any solution, and the eight-road maze of establishing responsibility.

For example, Frants Shetints (Franc Setinc), member of the Presidency of the Central Committee of the Slovenian Communist Party (League), wants to know how Kosovo manages its affairs, because he feels that he is the one who pays for it. "Togetherness does not mean some people spend, while all others pay. . . . Slovenia insists on knowing who spends how much, who reinvests, who manages, who contributes to all these debts, and how. . . . Life in the Federation demands precisely defined relations and behaviour rules . . . we have to behave as we agreed to . . . ." (*NIN*, October 24, 1982). And a disgruntled member of the Belgrade city party committee says: "Yugoslavia cannot survive if based on separate 'national socialisms'. . . elements of federalization create disintegrative tendencies in our society on every level." (*NIN*, October 3, 1982.)

Similar voices are also heard in Kosovo from Albanians who realize that particularism has brought troubles. The Chairman of the Management Committee of the Trepcha mines, Kosovo Albanian Hazmi Mikulovchi, asserted: "It

is easier to obtain prospecting rights for Trepcha in China,
Turkey, or Iran than in some of our republics. . . . Trepcha
is not the one that desires to be confined to Kosovo. . . . "
(*NIN*, October 25, 1981). And the President of the Prishtina Communist Party Committee, Asem Vlasi, says:
". . . not everything is good, but it is better than in 1981
. . . we need qualified people to come here, that is the only
way for us to develop," but notes that the well-known
enterprise, "Feronikel," advertised in all Yugoslav newspapers, offering excellent pay, but had only one response
(*NIN*, December 18, 1983). Two years earlier, Vlasi held
similar views (*NIN*, August 16, 1981): "For quite some
time we are facing the tendency of particularism. . . mostly propagated by the techno-political bureaucracy, but
this does not coincide with the interests of associated
labor [the workers did not by and large join the riots in
1981] . . . . We have clumsily encircled eight systems of
education, and made it impossible for the youth from one
region to continue their education in another republic.
we have raised thousands of barriers. . . . We have to start
from the premise that Yugoslavia is one natural community." Unfortunately, utterances of his type of Kosovo
Albanian have in the past been voices in the wilderness.

In the military sphere, the voice of the Yugoslav army
has also been heard in opposition to particularism. In an
interview, General Dane Chuich, Chairman of the Yugoslav Army Committee in the Yugoslav Communist Party,
said: "Kosovo events have shown once again that every
exclusivity in Yugoslavia, and every placing of restrictions
on outside interference can represent a danger for the
country as a whole." (*NIN*, July 25, 1982.) He did not
suggest the need of using military force, but military presence does demonstrate Belgrade's commitment to pre-
serving the Yugoslav union.

It is also necessary at least to call attention to the
question of Yugoslav-Albanian relations. Potentially, Albania could use its compatriots in Kosovo to destabilize

Yugoslavia. Albania's instigations in Kosovo, however, could easily lead to military confrontation, which neither country wants.

The reluctance of the central government, as well as that of Serbia, to intervene directly in Kosovo affairs, does not satisfy Yugoslavs who are eager and impatient to see a resolution of the problem. They are apprehensive lest Albania get involved, with unknowable consequences. They do not fear Albania itself, but they know that certain events could trigger a chain reaction which might be impossible to control. What they have in mind is some form of intervention by the Soviet Union or through surrogates (such as Bulgaria) or both. Yugoslavs are painfully aware of how certain events triggered two world wars in which they were involved, and they, as well as peoples of other countries, are understandably concerned that similar events could lead to a third world war, which would be worse than the other two.

Finally, the urgency of finding an answer to the Kosovo problem is dramatized by the human condition. For all concerned, this is the immediate challenge of Kosovo. Most, if not all, of the approaches to the question, including the belief that only a newly-established democratic political system could provide a satisfactory solution, suffer from a common attribute—a long-term point of view. Most people, however, live in the short-term. Those in pain and exasperation cry out for justice now. This is a burning issue to those Serbs for whom Kosovo is home and not just a psychological condition. To them, justice delayed is justice denied.

Chronology of Serbian and Montenegrin Rulers

## SERBIA

1168-1196—Nemanja, founder of Nemanjich dynasty
1196-1223—Stefan Prvovenchani (First-Crowned), second son of Nemanja
1223-1233—Radoslav, first son of Stefan
1233-1242—Vladislav, second son of Stefan
1242-1276—Urosh I, third son of Stefan
1276-1281—Dragutin, elder son of Urosh I
1281-1321—Milutin, younger brother of Dragutin
1321-1331—Stefan Dechanski (Urosh III), son of Milutin
1331-1355—Dushan (Stefan Urosh IV), son of Stefan Dechanski
1355-1371—Urosh V, son of Dushan
1372-1389—Prince Lazar (Hrebeljanovich)
1389-1427—Despot Stefan (Lazarevich), son of Lazar
1427-1456—Djurdje Brankovich, nephew of Despot Stefan
1456-1458—Lazar, son of Djurdj
1459-1804—Serbia under Turkish rule

* * * *

1804-1813—Karadjordje, founder of Karadjordjevich dynasty
1815-1839—Milosh Obrenovich, founder of Obrenovich dynasty
1839-1858—Alexander Karadjordjevich, son of Karadjordje
1858-1860—Milosh Obrenovich

1860-1868—Mihailo Obrenovich, son of Milosh
1868-1889—Milan Obrenovich, nephew of Milosh
1889-1903—Alexander Obrenovich, son of Milan
1903-1921—Petar I Karadjordjevich
1921-1934—Alexander I Karadjordjevich, son of Petar
1934-1941—Regency for Petar II Karadjordjevich, son of
Alexander

## MONTENEGRO
(center of Serbdom in 17th and 18th centuries)

1499—Last of Crnojevich family
1499-1697—Tribal chieftains and bishops rule under Ottoman Turks
1697-1735—Bishop Danilo, first effective opponent of
Turkish rule
1735-1781—Bishop Sava, cautious, timid, gave up power
twice
1750-1766—Bishop Vasilije
1767-1773—Shchepan Mali
1782-1830—Petar I Petrovich-Njegosh
1830-1851—Bishop Petar II Petrovich-Njegosh
1851-1860—Prince Danilo Petrovich-Njegosh, nephew of
Petar II
1860-1916—Prince Nikola Petrovich

# SELECTED BIBLIOGRAPHY

Amery, Julian. *Sons of Eagle.* London, 1948.

Avramovski, Zivko. "Italijanska okupacija Kosova," *Istorijski glasnik*, Vols. 2-3, 1964.

Basic, Milivoje. *Stare srpske biografije.* Belgrade, 1930.

Baskin, Mark. "Crisis in Kosovo," *Problems of Communism.* March-April, 1983.

Bozic, Ivan, et al. *Istorija Jugoslavije.* 2nd ed. Belgrade, 1973.

Culinovic, Ferdo. *Okupatorska podela Jugoslavije.* Belgrade, 1970.

Curcic, Slobodan. *Gracanica: King Milutin's Church and its Place in Late Byzantine Architecture.* University Park, Pa., 1979.

Curcija-Prodanovic, Nada. *Heroes of Serbia.* London, 1963.

Cvijic, Jovan. *Balkanski rat i Srbija.* Belgrade, 1912.

—————. *Balkansko poluostrvo i jugoslovenske zemlje.* Belgrade, 1922.

Dedijer, Vladimir. *Jugoslovensko-arbanski odnosi, 1939-1948.* Belgrade, 1948.

Dinic, Mihailo. *Srpske zemlje u srednjem veku.* Belgrade, 1978.

Djilas, Milovan. *Conversations with Stalin.* New York, 1962.

187

Djordjevic, Tihomir. *Iz Srbije Kneza Milosa.* Two vols. Belgrade, 1922, 1924.

Djordjevic, Dimitrije, ed. *The Creation of Yugoslavia, 1914-1918.* Santa Barbara, Ca., 1980.

Djordjevic, Vladan. *Arnauti i velike sile.* Belgrade, 1913.

—————. *Srbija i Turska, 1894-1897.* Belgrade, 1928.

Djuric, Vojislav. *Antologija narodnih junackih pesama.* Belgrade, 1965.

—————. *Icones de Yougoslavie.* Belgrade, 1961.

—————. *Vizantijske freske u Jugoslaviji.* Belgrade, 1975.

Drachkovitch, Milorad M., ed. *East Central Europe: Yesterday, Today, Tomorrow.* Stanford, Ca., 1982.

Ekmecic, Milorad. *Ratni ciljevi Srbije, 1914.* Belgrade, 1973.

Frasheri, Sami Bey. *Was war Albanien, was ist es, was wird es werden.* Vienna-Leipzig, 1913.

Gavrilovic, Mihailo. *Milos Obrenovic.* 3 vols. Belgrade, 1908, 1909, 1912.

Gopcevic, Spiridon. *Geschichte von Montenegro und Albanien.* Gotha, Germany, 1914.

Hadri, Ali. "Kosovo i Metohija u kraljevini Jugoslaviji," *Istorijski glasnik,* Vols. 1-2, 1967.

—————. "Nacionalno ugnjetavanje siptarske narodnosti i stav i borba KPJ za nacionalna prava Siptara za vreme stare Jugoslavije," *Gjurmine Albanologjike,* Vol. 2, 1965.

Hadzi-Vasiljevic, Jovan. *Arbanaska liga-arnautska kongra i srpski narod u turskom carstvu, 1878-1822.* Belgrade, 1909.

Harris, David. *A Diplomatic History of the Balkan Crisis of 1875-1878.* Stanford, Ca., 1936.

Hoxha, Enver. *The Titoites.* Tirana, 1982.

—————. *With Stalin: Memoirs.* Tirana, 1981.

Ivanovic, Milan. *Srednjevkovni spomenici Kosova: Monumentet mesjetare e Kosoves.* Belgrade, 1974.

Ivic, Aleksa. *Rodoslovne tablice srpskih dinastija i vlastele.* Novi Sad, 1928.

Jaksic, Grgur. *Iz novije srpske istorije.* Belgrade, 1953.

Jirecek, Konstantin and Radonic, Jovan. *Istorija Srba.* Two vols. Belgrade, 1952.

Jovanovic, Jovan. *Juzna Srbija od kraja XVIII veka do oslobodjenja.* Belgrade, 1938.

Jovanovic, Slobodan. *Druga vlada Milosa i Mihaila, 1858-1860.* Belgrade, 1923.

—————. *Vlada Milana Obrenovica.* 3 vols. Belgrade, 1934.

Kasanin, Milan. *Srpska knjizevnost u srednjem veku.* Belgrade, 1975.

Karadzic, Vuk Stefanovic. *Prvi i drugi srpski ustanak.* Belgrade, 1947.

Kerner, Robert J., ed. *Yugoslavia.* Berkeley, Ca., 1949.

Kostich, Lazo M. *Holocaust in the "Independent State of Croatia."* Chicago, Ill., 1981.

Lee, Michele. "Kosovo between Yugoslavia and Albania," *New Left Review.* July-August, 1983.

Lendvai, Paul. *Eagles in Cobwebs.* Garden City, N.Y., 1969.

Mackenzie, Muir and Irby, P. A. *Travels in the Slavonic Provinces of Turkey in Europe.* London, 1867.

Markovic, Sima. *Nacionalno pitanje u svetlosti marksizma.* Belgrade, 1923.

—————. *Ustavno pitanje i radnicka klasa Jugoslavije.* Belgrade, 1923.

Mihailovic, Konstantin. *Janicarove uspomene ili Turska Hronika.* Belgrade, 1959.

Mihailovich, Vasa D., ed. *Landmarks in Serbian Culture and History.* Pittsburgh, Pa., 1983.

Mijatovich, Elodie Lawton. *Kosovo.* London, 1884.

Millet, G. *Etudes sur les eglises de Rascie.* Paris, 1930.

Milosevic, S. *Izbeglice i preseljenici na teritorije okupirane Jugoslavije, 1941-45.* Belgrade, 1981.

Miskovic, Jovan. *Kosovska bitka.* Belgrade, 1890.

Novakovic, Stojan. *Zakonik Stefana Dusana, cara srpskog 1349 i 1354.* Belgrade, 1878.

Ostrogorsky, George. *History of the Byzantine State.* Rutgers, N.J., 1957.

—————. *Vizantija i sloveni.* Belgrade, 1975.

Panic-Surep, Milorad. *Kad su zivi zavideli mrtvima.* Belgrade, 1960.

Pano, Nicholas C. *The People's Republic of Albania.* Baltimore, 1968.

Paris, Edmond. *Genocide in Satellite Croatia, 1941-1945.* Chicago, Ill., 1962.

Pesic, Desanka. *Jugoslovenski komunisti i nacionalno pitanje, 1919-1935.* Belgrade, 1983.

Pavlovic, Miodrag. *Antologija srpskog pesnistva XIII-XX vek.* Belgrade, 1964.

Pavlowitch, Stevan K. *Yugoslavia.* London-New York, 1971.

Pavlowitch, Stevan K. and Biberaj, Elez. "The Albanian Problem in Yugoslavia: Two Views," *Conflict Studies.* London, 1982.

Petkovic, Vladimir R. *La penture Serbe du Moyen age.* Two vols. Belgrade, 1930, 1934.

———. *Pregled crkvenih spomenika kroz povesnicu srpskog naroda.* Belgrade, 1950.

Pollo, Stefanaq and Puto, Arben. *The History of Albania.* London, 1981.

Popovic, Dimitrije. *Borba za narodno ujedinjenje, 1908-1914.* Belgrade, 1936.

Popovic, Vasilj. *Evropa i srpsko pitanje u periodu oslobodjenja, 1804-1918.* Belgrade, 1938.

Radojcic, Svetozar. *Staro srpsko slikarstvo.* Belgrade, 1966.

———. *Srpske ikone od XII veka do 1459 godine.* Belgrade, 1960.

Ranke, Leopold. *Srpska revolucija.* Belgrade, 1965.

Redakcija za istoriju Crne Gore. *Istorija Crne Gore.* Titograd, 1967.

Rice, D. Talbot and Radojcic, S. *Yougoslavie, Fresques medieveles.* Paris, 1955.

Rusinow, Dennison. "Events in the SAP of Kosovo: Documentation," *Review of International Affairs.* Belgrade, 1981.

—————. "The Other Albania: Kosovo 1979," *American Universities Field Staff Report,* 1980.

Samardzic, Radovan. *Mehmed Sokolovic.* 2nd ed. Belgrade, 1975.

Shoup, Paul. *Communism and the Yugoslav National Question.* New York, 1968.

Skendi, Stavro. *The Albanian National Awakening, 1878-1912.* Princeton, N.J., 1967.

Slijepcevic, Djoko. *Istorija srpske pravoslavne crkve.* Two vols. Munich, 1962, 1966.

—————. *The Macedonian Question.* Chicago, Ill., 1958.

—————. *Srpsko-arbanaski odnosi kroz vekove, sa posebnim osvrtom na novije vreme.* 2nd ed. Himmelstur, West Germany, 1983.

Stankovic, Todor. *Beleske o Staroj Srbiji i Makedoniji.* Nis, 1915.

Stanojevic, Gligor. *Crna Gora pred stvaranje drzave, 1773-1779.* Belgrade, 1962.

—————. *Srbija u vreme beckog rata, 1683-1699.* Belgrade, 1976.

Stanojevic, Stanoje. *Istorija srpskog naroda u srednjem veku.* Belgrade, 1937.

Stewart, Cecil. *Serbian Legacy.* London, 1959.

Stojanovic, Ljubomir. *Stari srpski zapisi i natpisi.* 6 vols. Belgrade and Sremski Karlovci, 1902-1926.

Stojadinovic, Milan. *Ni rat ni pakt: Jugoslavija izmedju dva rata.* Buenos Aires, 1963.

Stojkovic, Ljubisa and Martic, Milos. *Nacionalne manjine u Jugoslavije.* Belgrade, 1953.

Sufflay, Milan. *Srbi i Arbanasi: njihova simbioza u srednjem veku.* Belgrade, 1925.

Tanjug. *Enver Hodzina Albanija.* Belgrade, 1981.

Temperley, Harold W. V. *History of Serbia.* London, 1919.

Tomic, Jovan. *O Arnautima u Staroj Srbiji i Sandzaku.* Belgrade, 1913.

—————. *Pecki patrijarh Jovan i pokret hriscana na Balkanskom poluostrvu, 1592-1614.* Zemun, 1903.

Tucovic, Dimitrije. *Srbija i Arbanija.* Belgrade, 1914.

Vucinich, Wayne S. *Serbia Between East and West: The Events of 1903-1908.* Stanford, Ca., 1954.

—————. *The First Serbian Uprising: 1804-1813.* New York, 1982.

Vukmanovic, Svetozar-Tempo. *Revolucija koja tece.* 2 vols. Belgrade, 1971.

West, Rebecca. *Black Lamb and Grey Falcon: A Journey through Yugoslavia.* New York (Penguin ed.), 1982.

Yugoslavia. *Bela Knjiga o Albansko-Jugoslovenskim odnosima, 1948-1961.* Belgrade, 1962.

**Periodicals and Newspapers** (among others)

*Borba*
NIN (*Nedeljne informativne novine*)
*Politika*
*Pravoslavlje*

# INDEX

Christians together against Turks
Palaeologus, Michael VIII—Byzantine emperor (1259-1282); cleared Constantinople of Latin control; established rule of dynasty, 2
Palfi—Vienna's envoy to Vatican, 110
Pano, Nicholas C.—134
Paraskeva—Mother Superior of Kosovo Devich monastery, 166-167
Paris, Edmond—138
Pashich, Nikola—Serbian politician and statesman (1845-1926); envoy to St. Petersburg (1893); Serbia's and Yugoslavia's prime minister intermittently until 1926, 100, 104-106, 110, 111, 114, 116
Pashich, Slad—57
Pavle (bishop)—171
Pech Patriarchate—monastery complex; See of Serbian archbishops and patriarchs (1346-1463) and (1557-1766), 40, passim
Petar Petrovich-Njegosh I—71, 76
Petar Petrovich-Njegosh II—Montenegrin bishop (ruled 1830-1851); poet and author, 79, 80
Peter the Great—Russian Tsar, 54, 70
Piccolomini—Austrian general, 65
Poll, Stefanaq—91-95
Popovich, Miladin—Yugoslav Communist organizer among Albanians, 145, 146, 148, 156, 159
Popovich, Dimitrije—103
Potiorek, Oscar—Austro-Hungarian general in World War I, 110
Prishtina—capital of Kosovo, population 135,000 (1981); Tsar Dushan's capital and in 19th century "city of consuls" (Austrian, Italian, Russian, Serbian)
Prishtina, Hasan—Kosovo Albanian political leader, 125

Prizren League—meeting held in 1878 of Moslem delegates alarmed by Slav upheaval in Balkans; considered cornerstone in process of Albanian national awakening, 91, 93, 95, 96, 177
Puto, Arben—91, 115

Radoslav—Serbian king (1223-1233) eldest son of Stefan the First-Crowned, 33
Rakich, Milan—Serbian poet, diplomat, 39
Ranke, Leopold von—German historian (1795-1886); introduced Serbia to Europe with his book, *Die Serbische Revolution,* 74
Rankovich, Alexander—leading Communist in Tito's Yugoslavia; expelled from ranks of party in 1966, 159
Rascia (Rashka)—Venetian term for Serbia
Rastko (St. Sava)—see Sava
Ravanitsa—monastery in Serbia built by Prince Lazar, 15, 26
Resava (Manasija)—monastery in Serbia, 15
Ristich, Serafim—95
Rizaj, Skender—professor, Prishtina University, editor of review, *Albanological Research,* 177
Rodofinikin, Konstantin—75
Rotulovich, Sinnan-Pashich—57
Rovine—battlefield in Romania where Prince Mircea fought valiantly against Bayazet, and where King Marko and Konstantin Dejanovich perished as Turkish vassals (1394), 15

Salisbury, Lord—92
Samardzich, Radovan—49
Samodrezha—historic church north of Prishtina, where Prince Lazar